Teaching, Learning and Assessment

D0121026

Teaching, Learning and Assessment

John Blanchard

Open University Press

Open University Press
McGraw-Hill Education
McGraw-Hill House
Shoppenhangers Road
Maidenhead
Berkshire
England
SL6 2QL

email: enquiries@openup.co.uk
world wide web: www.openup.co.uk

and Two Penn Plaza, New York, NY 10121-2289, USA

First published 2009

Copyright © John Blanchard 2009

All rights reserved. Except for the quotation of short passages for the purposes of criticism and review, no part of this publication may be reproduced, stored in a retrieval system, or transmitted, in any form, or by any means, electronic, mechanical, photocopying, recording or otherwise, without the prior permission of the publisher or a licence from the Copyright Licensing Agency Limited. Details of such licences (for reprographic reproduction) may be obtained from the Copyright Licensing Agency Ltd of Saffron House, 6–10 Kirby Street, London, EC1N 8TS.

A catalogue record of this book is available from the British Library

ISBN-13: 9780335233793 (pb)   9780335233809 (hb)
ISBN-10: 0335233791 (pb)   0335233805 (hb)

Library of Congress Cataloguing-in-Publication Data
CIP data applied for

Typeset by BookEns Ltd, Royston, Herts.
Printed in the UK by Bell & Bain Ltd, Glasgow.

Fictitious names of companies, products, people, characters and/or data that may be used herein (in case studies or in examples) are not intended to represent any real individual, company, product or event.

Mixed Sources
Product group from well-managed
forests and other controlled sources
www.fsc.org   Cert no. TT-COC-002769
© 1996 Forest Stewardship Council

The **McGraw·Hill** Companies

Contents

Acknowledgements

A number of sections in the book draw on three articles:

- for *The Curriculum Journal* (vol. 19, issue 3): 'Learning awareness: constructing formative assessment in the classroom, in the school and across schools', published by Taylor & Francis Group;
- for *Curriculum Briefing*: 'Listen up: giving feedback and evaluating progress', published by Optimus Publishing;
- for *The Cambridge Journal of Education*: 'Separating formative and summative assessment', awaiting publication.

This book reflects the commitment, energy and insight of many school pupils, teachers and leaders in Portsmouth. An enormous debt is also owed to Nick Brown (Student Voice consultant for the University of Sussex), Fiona Carnie (project manager), Fiona Collins (AfL team member for Portsmouth LA), Barbara Crossouard (AfL team member for the University of Sussex), Michael Fielding (project director), Ken Hann (LA contracted consultant for AfL), Mike Johns (LA adviser for AfL), Judy Sebba (research director) and Jo Thorp (AfL team member for the University of Sussex). Thanks to Harry Torrance for linking me up again with Michael. Special thanks to Ken Hann also for invaluable and painstaking commentary on most draft sections of the book, and for contributing notes and materials: he became my talk partner and peer assessor when the project team had to stop.

I wish to thank the headteachers, staffs, pupils and governors of these Portsmouth schools for their commitment, openness and insight:

Admiral Lord Nelson School
Arundel Court Junior School
Charles Dickens Junior School
City of Portsmouth Girls' School
Corpus Christi RC Primary School
Court Lane Infant School
Craneswater Junior School
East Shore School
  (now The Mary Rose School)
Gatcombe Park Primary School
Highbury Primary School
Isambard Brunel Junior School
Langstone Infant School
Manor Infant School

Arundel Court Infant School
Charles Dickens Infant School
City of Portsmouth Boys' School
College Park Infant School
Cottage Grove Primary School
Court Lane Junior School
Cumberland Infant School
Futcher School
  (now The Mary Rose School)
Goldsmith Infant School
Highlands-Spinnaker Centre
King Richard School
Langstone Junior School
Mayfield School

Medina Primary School
Meon Junior School
Miltoncross School
Milton Park Junior School
Northern Parade Infant School
Paulsgrove Primary School
Portsdown Primary School
Redwood Park School
St John's RC Primary School
St Luke's CE Secondary School
St Swithun's RC Primary School
Sevenoaks Centre
Solent Junior School
Southsea Infant School
Stamshaw Infant School
Waterside School
Westover Primary School
Wimborne Junior School.

Meon Infant School
Meredith Infant School
Milton Park Infant School
Moorings Way Infant School
Northern Parade Junior School
Penhale Infant School
Priory School
St Edmund's Catholic School
St Jude's C of E Primary School
St Paul's RC Primary School
Saxon Shore Infant School
Solent Infant School
Somers Park Primary School
Springfield School
Stamshaw Junior School
Westfield Junior School
Wimborne Infant School

I also wish to thank the following for specific contributions throughout the project:

Monica Bower, Sevenoaks Centre
Llyn Codling, Isambard Brunel Junior School
Rosie Dean, Springfield School
Eve Didwell, Solent Infant School
Pete Gilhooly, King Richard School
Iain Gilmour, Westfield, and Isambard Brunel, Junior Schools
Kathy Hawkins, Redwood Park School
Ben Hawksworth, Futcher and Mary Rose Schools
Amanda Hillyard, Admiral Lord Nelson School
Austen Hindman, Mayfield School
James Hobson, Springfield School
Anne Hounam, Waterside School
Carol House, Miltoncross School
James Humphries, Priory School
Dave Jordan, Springfield School
Shirley Kett, Cumberland Infant School
Steve Labedz, Admiral Lord Nelson School
Basil Lodge, Isambard Brunel Junior School
Bernard MacDonagh, Highland/Spinnaker Centre
June McFarlane, Springfield School
Georgina Mulhall, Solent Junior School

Beverly Naylor, Meredith Infant School
Graham O'Neil, City of Portsmouth Girls' School
Jonathan Russell, Springfield School
Marilyn Saunders, Craneswater Junior School
Rev Scammell, City of Portsmouth Girls' School
Linda Stallion, Langstone Infant School
Julie Stewart, East Shore and Mary Rose Schools
Carole Taylor, Meon Infant School
Katie Walker, City of Portsmouth Girls' School
Simon Watkins, King Richard School
Annette White, Meredith Infant School
Sue Wilson, Northern Parade Infant School
Daphne Wright, Portsdown Primary School
The Portsmouth Foundation Stage Advisory Team.

Thanks also go to:

Jacky Blanchard, Mandy Cox, Adam Darley, Natalie Tombs and Jo Wells,
Corfe Hills Technology College, Poole;
Jenny Coomber, Westfield Technology College, Weymouth, Dorset;
Teri Goodinson, St Mary's C of E Primary School, Beaminster, Dorset;
Dorothy Kavanagh, Oxfordshire County Council;
Avtar Singh Mangat, Jan Midgley and staff at Wilkes Green Junior School,
Birmingham;
Diane Martindale, Janet Rigby and staff at Christ Church Primary School,
Leigh, Wigan;
Elaine O'Connell, masters student with Plymouth University;
Montacute School, Poole, Dorset;
Priestlands School, Lymington, Hampshire;
Ringwood School, Ringwood, Hampshire;
Twynham School, Christchurch, Dorset.

I owe a debt of gratitude to Norman Schamroth, Ann Beer, Pete Rothman, their class, and headteacher Phil Minns, at Damers First School, Dorchester, Dorset. During the spring term 2008 Norman enabled me to test and refine these ideas about formative assessment by filming lessons and using examples from his inspirational practice. The filming project was helped by Mark Richardson and Peter Roe at Films for Learning (visit www.filmsforlearning. org).

Finally, thanks to Fiona Richman at Open University Press for focusing on the reader and suggesting important improvements.

Abbreviations and glossary

Abbreviations and acronyms appear in bold type at their first mention in the text.

AfL   Assessment for learning, also called formative assessment: aspects of pedagogy relating both to assessment and to the quality of teaching and learning outcomes.

AST   Advanced skills teacher: someone who has trained and been approved as a teacher able to coach and advise others in their own school and beyond.

CPD   Continuing professional development: training and study which informs teachers', leaders' and managers' performance management and career advancement.

CSIE   Centre for Studies in Inclusive Education: organization committed to investigating theory, policy and practice in education and its effects on the inclusion and exclusion of certain learners.

DCSF   Department for Children, Schools and Families: government department in England responsible for education.

DfES   Department for Education and Skills: earlier name for the government department in England responsible for education.

DES   Department of Education and Science and the Welsh Office: earlier name for the government department in England responsible for education.

DT   Design technology: a foundation subject in the English national curriculum.

EBI   Even better if . . .: a statement starter used in lessons to encourage learners to work out how to build on what they have done so far.

GCSE   General Certificate of Secondary Education: a main measure of educational outcomes at age 16 in England.

GTP   Graduate teacher programme: a route into the teaching profession for graduates or adults with equivalent experience and qualifications.

HMI   Her Majesty's Inspector of schools: the highest class of school inspector employed by the Office for Standards in Education in England.

ICT   Information communication technology: a core subject in the English national curriculum.

IEP   Individual education plan: a means of recording the planning and reviewing of a pupil's learning, also known as an individual learning plan or ILP. See also PDP.

ILP	Individual learning plan: see IEP, also PDP.
ILT	Information learning technology: alternative title for ICT, a core subject in the English national curriculum.
INSET	In-service training: opportunities for education professionals to develop their skill, knowledge and understanding.
ITT	Initial teacher training: a process by which someone gains access to the teaching profession in England.
IWB	Interactive white board: an information and communication technology facility used to support teaching and learning in many classrooms.
LA	Local authority: government, below national level, responsible for the administration of education for a county, urban area or borough.
LO	Learning objective: what someone wants pupils to achieve, also called a learning intention.
LSA	Learning support assistant: someone employed to assist teachers, often working with individual children or small groups of pupils in the classroom; see also TA.
MFL	Modern foreign languages: part of the national curriculum in England, comprising any one or more languages such as Mandarin, Spanish, Urdu, French, German …
MSC	Must, should, could: a way of setting different levels of challenge to a class, so that everyone must learn x, most should learn y, and some should try to go on to z.
NPQH	National Professional Qualification for Headship: a process by which someone gains access to recognized status as a candidate for headship in an English school.
NQT	Newly qualified teacher: the status given to teachers in their first year of teaching following initial teacher training in England.
Ofsted	Office for Standards in Education: the government agency responsible for inspecting schools and educational establishments.
PDP	Personal development plan: see IEP, also ILP.
PE	Physical education: an English national curriculum subject.
P-scales	Performance scales: statutory indicators of capability for children with learning difficulties or special educational needs who are working below level 1 of the national curriculum in England.
PSHE	Personal, social and health education, which includes citizenship.
QCA	Qualifications and Curriculum Authority: the governmental agency in Britain with a remit to develop the national curriculum and associated assessments, tests and examinations.
RE	Religious education: a statutory subject outside the English national curriculum, governed by locally agreed syllabuses.
SDP	School development plan: document which sets out priorities and

procedures for actions to be taken over a significant period of time (e.g. anything from one year to five years) with the effect of enhancing educational provision and outcomes. See also SIP.

SEAL   Social and emotional aspects of learning: the title given to a government initiative in England to emphasize holistic learning in a context that recognizes more than academic agendas.

SEF   Self evaluation form: the document used in England to record how a school rates itself, and inform the process of inspection.

SEN   Special educational needs: a classification which means a pupil requires some additional support.

SENCo   Special educational needs co-ordinator: person responsible for overseeing provision and outcomes for children judged to have special needs.

SIP   School improvement plan: document which sets out priorities and procedures for actions to be taken over a significant period of time (e.g. anything from one year to five years) with the effect of enhancing educational provision and outcomes. See also SDP.

SLT   Senior leadership team: colleagues including head and deputy headteachers responsible for vision, strategy, effectiveness and development.

TA   Teaching assistant: person employed to help teachers in the classroom and with other duties; see also LSA.

UoS   University of Sussex: higher education institution on the south coast of England.

WALT   We are learning to: a way of communicating learning intentions.

WILF   What I'm looking for: a way of focusing on the criteria for activity. In the early days of AfL it was taken for granted that the 'I' was the teacher, but some imaginative teachers have interpreted the 'I' in the learner's voice, making it what the learner is looking for in her/his activity.

Y   Year: as in Y4, the cohort in its fourth national curriculum year.

YR   Year reception: the reception class for school entrants around their fifth birthday in England.

ZPD   Zone of proximal development: the gap between what a learner can do now and capabilities that guidance, support and practice allow her/him to develop.

Ways to use this book

You can read from cover to cover.

You can skim-read for sections to concentrate on.

You can use Appendix 1 to take stock of your current formative assessment practices.

You can use Appendix 2 to chart your strengths and priorities from ten aspects of formative assessment.

You can start with lesson observations in Appendix 7.

You can use Chapter 14 on whole-school development.

You can compare your own experience with that of other schools, shown in Appendix 9.

You can choose which options from the 'Ten things to be clear about' to focus on (Chapters 4–13).

You can use, with acknowledgement, any of the sections in the book to inform meetings, working groups, or training activities.

You can do any combination of the above.

1 Getting started: a model for formative assessment

- Overview of the book
- An action research project: main findings
- Reflections on the project's outcomes

This first chapter answers the questions:

- What are the origins and focus of this book?
- What can we learn from the project behind this book?

Teaching, Learning and Assessment is a practical book for teachers and everyone interested in teaching. The focus is on teaching pupils to direct their own learning. This can include helping pupils to do well in tests and gain qualifications. But it goes far beyond that. Whole-school development is a theme. And there are important implications for policy, strategic leadership and government.

Overview of the book

This book deals with formative assessment, that is, assessment designed to inform and enhance pupils' learning. This can include assessing the quality of teaching, resources and the learning environment. It can include assessing the pupils' attitudes, motivations and readiness to tackle tasks. It is usually teachers, assistants and learners themselves who do the assessing in order to benefit current and future learning. It does not have to wait till the end of a course, nor be carried out under controlled conditions. It does not have to involve writing, nor be sent away to be marked with a delay of several months before results are known. It does not have to be recorded, stored, or monitored. It has to be quality assured only insofar as teaching and learning are.

Assessment is traditionally summative, which means making judgements about how well pupils have learned what they should have been taught. Judgements are made by authorized examiners and teachers acting as examiners. The function of summative assessment is to maintain standards by which examinees are qualified, and report results.

> The function of formative assessment is not to report results, but to improve the processes and outcomes of learning. Formative assessment questions how pupils learn, why they have the curriculum they have, and how they are helped or hindered by their provision. This is a profound and extensive challenge, consistent with an agenda of inclusive education.

The summative model of assessment is linear and separates out the three elements: first there is teaching; then there is learning; finally there is assessment. The formative model is complex and dynamic in comparison. These assessments take place during teaching, as part of the learning. *Teaching, Learning and Assessment* has all three working together.

For some teachers there is an irreconcilable conflict between formative and summative assessments. They say that preparing pupils for tests and exams makes it all but impossible to develop their independence. If you feel formative assessment is incompatible with results and raising standards, this book should be of interest. I aim to show that *how* you help your pupils meet public criteria has other benefits, including increasing their collaboration, critical and creative thinking, and confidence.

Processes of formative assessment were given a clear and practical definition by the Assessment Reform Group (2002), as:

> seeking and interpreting evidence for use by learners and their teachers to decide where the learners are in their learning, where they need to go and how best to get there.

So it is not just you, but your pupils also, who can do the assessing. This book offers guidance as to *how* learners and teachers might use assessment to decide current capability and the way ahead. In the process there may be implications for public policy and strategy.

There are few simple solutions to the challenges of assessment in teaching and learning. There are no guarantees or panaceas, because the contexts are too variable. But we do learn from experience and theory.

The requirements, structures and conditions, which leaders and managers are responsible for, have an impact on what you and your pupils find feasible and worthwhile. I want this book to help you in your dealings with governing authorities.

> The teaching at the centre of this book aspires to support learners' growing autonomy. It emphasizes learning together and from one another. It aims to foster positive attitudes about learners' abilities and about the nature of ability. It indicates that pupils' learning about learning provides a model for professionals' and schools' development.

You should find this relevant whatever the age of your pupils. The examples and recommendations relate as much to the reception class and early years as to special, primary, secondary school and post-16 settings.

The ideas and practices presented here relate to every curriculum subject, including personal, social and health education (**PSHE**). Though literacy and numeracy are prominent, the sciences, arts, humanities, technology, religious and physical education offer outstanding illustrations of formative assessment.

All of this applies to a range of settings: lessons; in-service (**INSET**) and initial teacher training (**ITT**); continuing professional development (**CPD**); team development; and whole-school improvement, reflected in the school development plan (**SDP**) and self-evaluation form (**SEF**).

The ideas and practices presented here grow out of and build on my teaching, advisory teaching and, most recently, my work as a consultant to schools, local authorities and higher education institutions. Chief amongst these has been the experience of a partnership between Portsmouth Local Authority (**LA**), schools and centres in the city, and the Centre for Educational Innovation at the University of Sussex (**UoS**). Although I have no brief to represent those who contributed to the learning community, I am trying to pass on what we learned and so use the plural 'we' when a collective voice seems warranted.

Chapter 2 explores the role of learners' interest in lesson activities. Chapter 3 presents a model of 'transparency' and 'interactivity' and a framework of 'Ten things to be clear about' in teaching and learning. These give terms of reference for a shift that can be made in the direction of greater participation by learners in decision-making about lessons and in their assessment.

Chapters 4 to 13 offer practical ways into decisions that determine the quality of teaching and learning in lessons. You do not have to take them in order. You can confirm areas of practice that you feel confident about, and choose what to explore and develop. Each of these options contains:

- what teachers, pupils and leaders have learned about using formative assessment to enhance teaching and learning;
- prompts to help you reflect on your practice;
- activities and steps to take;
- signs of moving from transparent to interactive teaching and learning;
- ways of taking professional and whole-school development forward.

It is unlikely that all of the material here will be new to you. The idea behind this structure is for you to recognize strengths in your current teaching and learning and find what you need to stimulate and guide further development. The intention is not that you necessarily cover all ten elements. The direction and momentum you gain from exploring a small number of the options will carry over into all aspects of your attitude and approach.

I recommend you choose to promote areas where you already have some experience. Rather than starting with matters you feel least expert in, you can work on strategies you wish to bring up to the level of your greatest strengths.

Chapter 14 gives an overview of approaches to continuing professional development and whole-school improvement. Chapter 15 focuses on how formative and summative assessments differ. Chapter 16 describes how the project behind this book was carried out, and sets it in a research context.

The appendices provide practical materials: checklists, guidelines, lesson observations and case studies.

Throughout I use certain terms more or less interchangeably. 'Learning objectives' and 'learning intentions' are what it is hoped lessons will achieve. 'Success criteria', 'quality criteria' and 'assessment criteria' define features of what is being looked for. 'Learners' may be 'pupils' or 'students', 'children' or 'young people'. And so on.

Now here is some information about the project behind this book. It ran from 2002 to 2007 as part of the Portsmouth Learning Community, which had three strands: assessment for learning (**AfL**, or formative assessment); colleagues' learning from one another across institutional boundaries ('school-to-school learning'); and pupils having a voice in educational decision-making ('student voice').

An action research project: main findings

About a year into the project we developed a model, which we modified at regular intervals. We saw that in its early stages assessment for learning tends to affirm or introduce 'transparency', and, given certain values and circumstances, this can grow into 'interactivity'. Both are an advance on prescriptive and autocratic cultures.

In our view, when teachers make transparent such things as purposes and criteria for activities in lessons, they provide useful guidance. When they enable learners to play an interactive part in deciding such things, teachers help learners to be resilient and reflective. Clarity is the first step. Shared decision-making is the second step.

Leaders and managers who create conditions which support transparency or interactivity in professional and institutional development, are most effective in promoting the same conditions for pupils' learning.

Interactive pupils and colleagues learn to:

- help, and be helped by, those around them;
- accept, even welcome, difficulty, trial and error;
- have their own sense of purpose and progress;

- improve their performance and transfer their learning.

They are enabled to develop these qualities by interactive teachers, leaders and managers who:

- present themselves as fallible, learning with their pupils/colleagues;
- adapt their teaching/ways of working to how their pupils/colleagues respond;
- want their pupils/colleagues to direct their own learning/development as far as possible.

Though they may know what to do, pupils in a transparent classroom, like colleagues in a transparent institution, present themselves as passive and dependent, waiting to be spoon-fed or told what to do. Pupils in an interactive classroom, like colleagues in an interactive institution, tend to act with a confident sense of purpose on agendas that are agreed with or acceptable to their teachers or institutional leaders and managers. Reliance on authority can become readiness to think and act responsibly and with initiative.

It is the quality of their relationship and dialogue with teachers and leaders that determines how much pupils and staff members decide. As a junior school teacher said, *AfL is something you are, not something you do.* And a secondary pupil, *I don't want a teacher who influences me. I want a teacher who teaches me not to be influenced.*

We developed our model as a way of understanding what otherwise are mere mechanics:

- planning for *learning* rather than merely *doing*;
- deciding how to work together and how to organize the classroom/ space/resources (groundrules and ethos);
- reviewing what we already know (recapping), and deciding what we might want to learn (mind-mapping);
- making objectives visible, and referring to them;
- clarifying what the pupils *must*, *should* and *could* try to achieve (differentiation);
- having individual and/or group targets;
- seeing how this topic links with others (the 'big picture');
- exploring why this might be important to learn (the rationale);
- defining what counts as good (criteria);
- making criteria visible, and referring to them;
- knowing what steps to take (having a clear method);
- having models to work from;
- using talk partners and helping one another;

- everyone having time to think about answers to questions;
- asking fewer yes/no questions and more open questions;
- seeing how difficulties and mistakes can help learning (developing resilience and perseverance);
- discussing what helps and what hinders learning;
- having positive feedback referring to objectives and criteria;
- self assessment and peer assessment (e.g. using markschemes);
- highlighting successes and strengths;
- having time and guidance to improve performance and develop learning (doing corrections, revisions and extension work);
- taking a teaching role;
- discussing how learning can be applied in other contexts.

(Also shown in Appendix 1.)

You can identify which of these methods you already use. Be aware that techniques cannot guarantee to raise the quality of learning. Formative assessment goes much deeper than the implementation of this or that teaching device.

We identified ten main focuses that make a difference to teachers' and learners' experience. The most effective leaders and teachers make these things explicit *and* enable pupils and colleagues to share decision-making about them.

Ten things to be clear about

[1] How do we work together?
e.g. groundrules; think-time; learning partners; deciding and choosing; helping one another; being treated as an individual; being open about not knowing

[2] What do we know about this topic?
e.g. recapping; mind-mapping; learning walls

[3] What are we trying to achieve?
e.g. focus on learning; key questions; big picture; targets; displays

[4] What might be interesting about this?
e.g. fun; play; relevance; challenge; purpose

[5] How can we know how well we do?
e.g. criteria for assessment/quality/success

[6] How do we tackle it?
e.g. modelling; checklist; roles; timings

[7] What can we do when we get stuck or go wrong?
e.g. routines; posters; learning partners; talking about how mistakes can help; talking about what 'ability' is

[8] What have we achieved?

e.g. products, presentations and exhibitions; self-checking; feed-back; using criteria to highlight strengths; traffic lighting

[9] How can we improve?

e.g. self-checking; comment marking; giving time for improvement; extending

[10] How can we use what we learn?

e.g. transferring skills and knowledge across subjects; relevance to life; teaching someone else

These can be summarized as follows:

Chapter 4:   Ethos
Chapter 5:   Prior knowledge
Chapter 6:   Intention
Chapter 7:   Interest
Chapter 8:   Criteria
Chapter 9:   Method
Chapter 10:   Resilience
Chapter 11:   Achievement
Chapter 12:   Improvement
Chapter 13:   Application

When teachers or leaders make things clear, the culture of the classroom or school tends to be transparent. When pupils or staff members make things clear for themselves and with one another, the culture tends to be interactive.

> Our project found that the distinctive quality of outstanding, inter-active lessons was not so much the use of this or that AfL method. Rather, it was the openness or closedness on the part of the teacher or authority towards learners' or stakeholders' options and initiatives. Associated with this, we found collaborative enquiry and experiment essential to transitions from transparency to interactivity.

If interactivity is the goal, learners have to become more and more active in decision-making. And this has to be informed and accompanied by teachers' and assistants' being active in decision-making about their own and their school's development. As a secondary school teacher noted:

> *The culture of reflection and evaluation that has been developed amongst the staff directly parallels the culture that senior leaders and teachers want to see amongst the pupils.*

We found that as much as teachers and learners in lessons need to be guided and evaluated by criteria that match their objectives, so too do leaders and managers in schools need to be guided and evaluated by criteria that match their objectives. In England these objectives are set out by *Every Child Matters* (**DfES**, 2003). Our conclusion was that the criteria currently used to judge lessons and educational outcomes are much narrower than the objectives pupils, teachers and schools have. The most confident schools in our project made case studies to illustrate the breadth of their progress and achievements. These appear in SEFs, CPD and SDPs. There is a vast apparatus of public administration overseeing the production of such documentation, all of which is ultimately stripped down to a league table position. This book tries to support the development of more appropriate systems.

Reflections on the project's outcomes

AfL's benefits appeared to extend beyond raising attainment as portrayed by end-of-key-stage cohort statistics. The Portsmouth Learning Community's final report (Fielding et al., 2008) reflected achievement in quantitative and qualitative terms. For 2005 and 2006, value-added scores at Key Stages 2 and 4 and progress measures from Key Stage 3 to **GCSE** showed 'good improvement in the progress made by students aged from 11 to 16' (p. 17). Additionally, in 'many schools, increases in attendance rates, decreases in exclusions and improvements in teaching were accepted as 'proxies' for raising standards in the longer term and school staff were encouraged by these shorter term outcomes' (p. 47). (Detailed accounts are given elsewhere: see Blanchard, 2006a and 2006b, and Appendix 9 here.)

> Colleagues and pupils reported that confidence, independence, peer cooperation and learning about learning, as well as attainment in terms of subject criteria, were boosted by AfL. Such indications were collected, for example, in SEFs, a scan of which showed that schools judged AfL to have contributed to the achievement of all five Every Child Matters outcomes: health, security, enjoyment and achievement, community contribution and economic well-being.

The enabling culture we came to define as interactive has much in common with the concept of inclusion, as promoted, for example, by the Centre for Studies in Inclusive Education (**CSIE**; see Tony Booth and Mel Ainscow, 2002). Judy Sebba and Mel Ainscow (1996: 9) have given this very helpful definition:

Inclusion describes the process by which a school attempts to respond to all pupils as individuals by reconsidering its curricular organization and provision. Through this process, the school builds its capacity to accept all pupils from the local community who wish to attend and, in so doing, reduces the need to exclude pupils.

This is consistent with our construction of formative assessment and interactive teaching and learning. A primary school special needs co-ordinator (**SENCo**) recently gave me a fine example of inclusiveness, which illustrates many of the features of interactivity:

It is hard to demonstrate: you have to see the interaction between the children to see how valuable it is. We have one class which contains two children with autism. What the others have learned is incredible: about tolerance; that there are different ways of learning; about difference. They have become a class that are able to support each other and work with their own initiative. If there is a problem, they can solve it. For example, when one child had a problem, we all sat down together and asked 'How can we help?' They came up with brilliant ideas and understanding: they have the generosity and imagination. And as a teacher I have benefited hugely, thinking about other ways of learning and other ways of engaging interest. We have to because we need to include all the children. It takes you back to basics and you have to change your whole way of teaching. It is beneficial for all.

Conventional assessment measures do not adequately reflect learners' inclusive and interactive achievement. We have to look to personal testimony, professional records and artefacts arising from the teaching and learning. There are many groups and organizations committed to this kind of work. Providing creative and documentary evidence, for example, is FilmsforLearning (visit www.filmsforlearning.org):

- We think that students know what engages other students.
- We want students to be excited by the creativity of their learning.
- We want students to work out what 'student voice' means.

We shared those convictions, and concluded that assessment succeeds in being formative when it enables learners to:

- understand how to judge what they achieve;
- understand how others can judge what they achieve;
- want to take their learning further;
- understand how to take their learning further.

These are criteria which can be used to evaluate the intrinsic effectiveness of any method or instance of would-be formative assessment. Extrinsic measures of effectiveness refer conventionally to summative assessment results, though more qualitative indicators and personal testimony can be considered.

Our findings mirrored almost identically those of the Secondary National Strategy 'Assessment for Learning and Schools Project Report' (**DfES**, 2007), insofar as extrinsic measures are concerned:

> Schools in the project found the impact of AfL on standards the most difficult to find evidence of (p. 29).

> Five (out of the eight) schools were able to evidence the impact of the quality of AfL practice in specific subjects on the progress and results in those subjects (p. 32).

> Four (out of the eight) schools could evidence the impact of the quality of AfL practice on groups of pupils taught by specific teachers (p. 32).

The National Strategy project's conclusions closely matched our own, insofar as intrinsic evidence is admitted:

> Pupils need to move from being passive recipients of what they are being taught, to develop as independent learners who take responsibility for their own learning and are empowered to make progress for themselves (p. 10).

> Leadership is neither 'top down' nor 'bottom up'. With distributed leadership comes shared ownership of, and contribution to, a continually evolving vision of where the school is going and how to get there (p. 12).

Our recommendations are in accord with those of the Teaching and Learning in 2020 Review Group (DfES, 2006: 39) that:

> The government should take further action to ensure that assessment for learning is embedded in all schools and classrooms so that its benefits are fully realized ...

> Schools should identify their own strategies for embedding assessment for learning, reporting regularly to governing bodies on their implementation and effectiveness.

Schools' and government's response has been positive. Policy and funding in England are directed toward *The Assessment for Learning Strategy* (the *Strategy* hereafter; **DCSF**, 2008). Whether this initiative will help schools to be proactive, or whether it will confirm dependence on government agencies, remains to be seen. Neither making the move from passive recipient to independent learner, nor making the move to shared leadership, can be imposed or dictated.

There is a danger in all of this that distribution of responsibility and authority fails to take place. There are ominous signs in the *Strategy* of a reversion to assessment *of* learning and a failure to grasp assessment *for* learning. It casts the learner in a willing-compliance but ultimately done-unto role: 'Pupils engaged in their learning and given immediate feedback' (p. 6). How to enable learners as well as schools to become autonomous remains a challenge.

Colleagues in our project lost any illusion about formative assessment being easy. As a secondary school teacher reflected, two years down the road:

> *Assessment for learning is actually a bit more of a revolution than people have been letting on. Since we met last, that is my new thinking. What we have here is not some interesting modifications, which I thought it was. It's actually a lot more profound than that. Because if you follow this through, then you end up with totally different things happening in the classroom. It's not tinkering any more.*

Our proactive senior leaders saw that changes in lessons had to be mirrored by changes in the culture of professional and whole-school development. A secondary deputy headteacher made this clear:

> *The key is a firm belief in empowering staff. If you want to effect change and it's a done-unto, it's not going to happen. If it's a done-with and done-by, then you're going to engage. It's the negotiation, parallel with the pupils' self- and peer assessment.*

Those who advocate and direct projects designed to improve education often underestimate the enduring effort to maintain, let alone develop, teaching and learning. As one of our primary school teachers put it:

> *It can't happen overnight. There are new members of staff, and there are learning support assistants who have not had the benefit of courses or special training, and they need opportunities to learn more about the school's aims and ways of working. The development process takes time, not least because at different times teachers may need just to cope or to consolidate.*

And as the secondary deputy headteacher, quoted above, said:

> *The day I take the perfect AfL lesson I shall probably retire!*

Further details about the project are given in Chapter 16.

2 Formative assessment needs interesting activity

- Looking for interest
- Self-image and attitude
- Giving activity meaning

In this chapter I summarize and paraphrase some outstanding research, answering the questions:

- How do you engage learners' interest?
- How important to pupils' learning is what they think they are doing?

The message is that, if learners are not interested, they are unlikely to be able to apply outside the teaching or testing situation what they learn in school. It is a significant challenge to make the activities you offer appeal to *and* have a lasting effect on your pupils.

Looking for interest

Albert Bandura's summary of international research (1997) gives a list of what effective teachers do to make educational activities accessible and engaging. They:

- make activities enjoyable;
- create personal challenges through goal setting;
- add variety to counteract boredom;
- encourage personal responsibility for achievements;
- provide feedback for progress.

Margaret Carr (2004) shows how certain kinds of task stimulate and sustain learning:

Tasks which are ...	help pupils to ...
- interesting and authentic	make connections with their lives
- accessible and transparent	see the point and become deeply involved for long periods

- challenging   stick at it and enjoy being puzzled
- collaborative   bounce ideas off one another
- multi-faceted   develop their talents for colour,
                         drawing, design, technology, making,
                         reasoning, number, measuring

So good lessons allow learners both to express the interior world of their imaginations and to explore the exterior world of things, nature and human affairs. Dialogue and choice are indispensable to this.

In keeping with this are the results of Mihalyi Csikszentmihalyi's extensive research overview (1991), revealing that we are fully engaged and have a feeling of 'flow', when we:

- have clear goals;
- get immediate feedback;
- sense the challenge is feasible;
- concentrate;
- are in the here and now;
- don't worry about failure;
- are not self-conscious;
- lose track of time;
- enjoy what we're doing for its own sake.

Self-image and attitude

Suspension of self in activity promotes learning. This demands, then repays, self-confidence, allied with trust in the environment and companions. Carol Dweck's research (2000) shows how important mindset is:

> When people have a contingent sense of self-worth, they feel like worthy people only when they have succeeded, and they feel deficient or worthless when they fail ... (p. 114)

> Self-esteem is how you feel when you are striving whole-heartedly for worthwhile things; it's how you experience yourself when you are using your abilities to the fullest in the service of what you deeply value ... (p. 128)

Approximately half of the respondents in Dweck's research give a view of ability as something fixed and innate, while the other half believe human beings have potential to grow through learning. Failing in a task tends to make the first group stop trying and feel worthless, or they ignore negative feedback and persevere in error. The second group accepts difficulty as something to be overcome.

When they make a mistake or are stuck, those who think ability is a once-and-for-all gift may ask for help, but they want the helper to take over. This is what Dweck calls 'learned helplessness'. By contrast, those who believe they can learn tend to keep trying and try something different.

Here we have two contrasting senses of security. Those with a fixed view of ability feel a kind of security provided there is someone there to rescue them and magically make everything right. Those who see ability as something they can shape for themselves feel secure in their own capability and responsibility.

Your challenge is to find ways of helping learners who make negative statements, such as those down the left-hand column below, to move towards being able to make the kinds of positive statement that appear in the right-hand column. You can affirm the resilience of those who already make the right-hand kind of statement:

I can't do it.	→	*Let's try again.*
Can you do this for me?	→	*Let me check.*
I'm no good at this.	→	*I haven't done this before.*
I don't like this. It's boring.	→	*This is hard. I like this.*
I give up.	→	*How else can I try this?*
I'll never be any good.	→	*I'm going to crack this.*
This is too easy for me.	→	*Is there more to this?*
I usually do harder work.	→	*I've done my best on this; what do you think?*

Giving activity meaning

The way pupils look at classroom work is bound up with how they perceive themselves. You can act on both by fostering a constructive self-image at the same time as offering worthwhile activities in the form of:

- finding out
- exploring
- rehearsing
- making
- presenting

When they are finding out, they listen, look, ask and read, for example:

- deciding what they think is worth investigating;
- identifying what they know and what they don't know;
- learning how to think of, frame and develop questions, e.g. interviewing, questionnairing, interrogating texts, planning projects based on enquiry;
- learning where to look for information, and how to look for it, using people nearby, libraries, the internet, indexing systems, etc.

When they are exploring, they research, experiment, imagine and analyse, for example:

- looking at familiar things in new ways;
- looking at unfamiliar things without fear;
- pushing and redefining boundaries: e.g. rethinking what they think is possible, what they think is good;
- criticizing and evaluating: e.g. seeing what is good and what can be improved in their own or someone else's performance.

When they are rehearsing, they repeat, practise, revise and train, for example:

- identifying and practising techniques and sub-routines that make up a performance;
- preparing for making or presenting – revising, drafting, prototyping;
- visualizing – using the image of an ideal performance as a guide and motivator;
- getting feedback from a coach or critic.

When they are making, they play, design, create and record, for example:

- considering what other people have done in the same field;
- expressing something of themselves in what they do;
- enjoying participation or production;
- deciding how they will treat feedback and comment.

When they are presenting, they give a talk or performance, make a display, broadcast and teach, for example:

- adapting presentation to purpose, audience and relevant conventions;
- offering an experience for others to enjoy, and if possible getting the benefit of their response.

You can check some of your current planning, and estimate the proportions of time your pupils will spend finding out, rehearsing, exploring, making and presenting. You can likewise monitor any lesson or sequence of lessons as it takes place: what is the balance between the different types of activity; what is the progression; what is the goal? You can modify the planning you next do to take account of these considerations, and give learning the emphases you intend.

> The quality of your teaching depends on the extent to which you plan, run and evaluate your lessons so that your pupils, rather than you, are the prime agents. Your objective can be that they take as much initiative and responsibility for their activities as possible.

This means reducing to a minimum the kind of 'activity' we might call 'doing classroom learning'. Typical of traditional lessons are the kinds of ritual whereby pupils answer questions or perform actions for the teacher's sake: as a demonstration of what they know and can do, not because they are interested and engaged in genuine problem-solving, enquiry, creativity or communication.

Learners can have an authentic sense of what they are doing and why they are doing it. They can define what they are doing for themselves: e.g. *I'm planning a story about my visit to a village in India, We're seeing how many ways there are to arrange cubes.* They can give their own reasons for what they are doing: e.g. *I'm including a range of sentence starters, I'm enjoying imagining, I want to show _____ what I can do, We're going to use this in an assembly for the rest of the school.*

The implication may be that alternative educational methods, contexts and partners need to be developed. Donald McIntyre (2003) asked sharp questions:

> Has classroom teaching served its day? ... Why is it that, despite 30 years of propaganda, teachers appear to make little use of formative assessment in their classroom practice? Is it ... because there has not been sufficient external encouragement and support for such good practice? A more plausible hypothesis might be that regular effective formative assessment so adds to the complexity of classroom teaching as to make it an impracticable option for teachers [under conventional circumstances] (p. 104)

This book is dedicated to finding ways of making formative assessment a practical proposition.

Some commentators believe schools will have to change more than the conduct of lessons if they are to meet modern learners' and society's needs.

McIntyre foresaw greater collaboration between teachers and other providers, more openness about the craft and direction of teaching, and greater variety in where teaching and learning are located. His prognosis can be summarized as follows:

Now	**In the future**
Who makes decisions about lessons?	
The teacher alone	The pupils and others (e.g. teaching assistants) with the teacher
How are decisions made?	
Mostly intuitively, tacitly, and privately	Collaboratively, explicitly, and in a more evidence-based way, as well as intuitively
Where does learning take place?	
In the classroom and instructional spaces	In other social groups and settings, as well as classrooms

Formative assessment probably needs to be seen as belonging to wider educational reforms. Very interesting examples are the Royal Society for the Encouragement of the Arts' 'Opening Minds' programme (2002) and the Arts Council England's 'Creative Partnerships' (see website, www.creative-partner ships.com).

In the meantime, your pupils' learning can be stimulated by building in dynamic qualities. Here are some examples:

- moving from one receptive or expressive mode to another: now listening, now speaking, now drawing, now reading;
- using DARTs (Directed Activities Related to Texts: e.g. see the Portsmouth Ethnic Minority Achievement Service website, www.blss. portsmouth.sch.uk), which challenge learners to translate information from one genre or language register and manner of presentation to another, such as changing a table of data into an explanatory paragraph, a cartoon into a short story, a discursive account into a diagram;
- periodically comparing their own intentions and efforts with models of others' performance: studying what others have done gives something to aspire to and/or something to critique and improve;
- alternating between working with a coach or mentor and working without; sometimes working with a self-chosen partner, sometimes with a partner chosen by you;

- switching from solo working to paired activity, from small group to whole-class work, and back to pairs: giving variety and momentum;
- taking a range of roles: now observer, now demonstrator; now researcher, now reporter; now coach, now critic.

These kinds of dynamism can convey to your pupils a vital sense that they are getting somewhere.

Wanting to learn something can be a real reason for wanting to carry out lesson activities. Other reasons include being drawn in by the appeal of the topic or activity, and enhancing personal satisfaction or social standing. My summary is that learners' interest is attracted and sustained by lessons which incorporate certain features and potentials.

Interesting lessons have these 'hooks' and attractions:

- puzzles or mysteries to be solved;
- imagination, play or creativity;
- varied, not monotonous, tasks and elements;
- active and productive, not merely passive and reproductive, tasks and elements;
- visual and physical, as well as literal and linguistic, tasks and elements.

Interesting lessons enable learners to:

- attach personal and social significance to activity, such that they realize opportunities to:
  - add to their repertoire of skill, knowledge and understanding;
  - prove something or fulfil personal ambitions;
  - please or impress another/others;
  - be like or different from others;
- accept as a context and reason for activity:
  - education, i.e. opportunity or requirement to conform or excel and gain knowledge and skill;
  - a real, or as-if real, scenario with relevance to their own pre-occupations and aspirations in current or prospective leisure and employment;
- experience:
  - adventure or independence;
  - control over details, framing or directing of activities;
  - collaborative and communicative, as well as solo and introverted, phases;
  - growing resilience and resourcefulness;
  - a sense of achievement through effort;

- gain:
  - through comparisons between existing and new capabilities, an enhanced sense of self;
  - through connections with personal interests and matters of work- and world-related relevance, enhanced enjoyment, empowerment and prospects.

A key question is who decides, who is in control. Pupils are much more likely to persevere if they take ownership of what they do. This is promoted by their being clear about crucial factors that shape and guide their activities. This is explored in the next chapter and through Chapters 4 to 13. Chapter 15 analyses how formative and summative assessments contrastingly affect interest in lessons.

3 Ten things to be clear about in teaching and learning

- 'Transparency' and 'interactivity' in classrooms and schools
- Helping to make important decisions

This chapter answers the questions:

- How is having things made clear different from taking part in decision-making?
- What sorts of decision can you and your pupils make?

This is the main focus of this book: how you can help learners pause for thought. Here assessment is synonymous with reflection, often involving dialogue. Reflection is a feature of planning, launching, adjusting and evaluating activity.

The previous chapter was concerned with action and cognition in action, and with having authentic reasons for carrying out activities in lessons. This chapter is about metacognition: thinking about action and cognition. It is about meanings that learners can give activity. This sets the scene for the next ten chapters.

The better you enable your pupils to think about what they do, the better they perform, the better they learn, and the better they feel about themselves.

This has to do with 'higher order' thinking skills, and these are not just for the 'more able' or 'gifted and talented' pupils. While it is true that thinking about what they do will enable some pupils to attain the highest academic standards, reflectiveness and imagination belong to all learners. Having a plan, trying hard, seeing results, interpreting and reasoning: all of these depend on metacognition, which is a defining human trait.

All learners can become clear about what they do, and so learn how to learn. The question is: how can they be helped to do so?

'Transparency' and 'interactivity' in classrooms and schools

As described in Chapter 1, the team I worked with on the Portsmouth

Learning Community Assessment for Learning project developed a model to explore some important differences between schools. In some, assessment was very much in the teachers' hands. In others, the pupils were just as involved, raising questions about the purpose, method, criteria, success and improvement of activities.

Pupils said they liked being informed about objectives, criteria, ways of improving, and so on. But they liked even more playing an active part in deciding some of these things with the teacher, with assistants, with one another and for themselves.

> Clarity about purpose, method, progress, and so on, is a first step towards involvement and fulfilment. Participation in decision-making is the second step.

Pupils and colleagues illustrated this in what they said.

Primary school teacher: *We had a lesson specifically on problem solving in maths, discussing 'What do you need to know?' The pupils came up with a list, and then we discussed 'How do you do each of those things?' This gave a focus to the teaching, and in my marking I could refer to the list, using the pupils' words. All of this fits together: the success criteria, the teaching, the marking, the talking with pupils at their table groups, and so on.*

Junior school teacher: *The pupils asked for the jotter, a book to write things in. So we have given the children jotting books, unsure about exactly how these would be used, inviting the children to jot down whatever they find helpful. One girl straightaway transferred all my comments in her English book into her jotter. Another wrote out her tables which she finds difficult. It could be more structured, but by whom? Ownership is crucial: so much of what the pupils experience in school is dictated. One pupil beamed from ear to ear, chuffed to have the jotter.*

Primary school pupils: *The success criteria are useful. It gives you confidence as you know you are doing it right.*

We use thumbs up to show we have understood.

We underline where we think we have done well.

We have to think about how the lesson was sometimes. It's good because you get to say if you're stuck.

At the end of the lesson we say how we felt about what we were doing, and this is good because she knows what we've got to do more work on.

We thought of the questions so we know what we've got to write.

We sometimes read out the bit we are most pleased with, and we get comments back from the rest of the class.

We developed our model to focus attention on the decision-making that teachers and assistants can help learners engage in. At issue is teachers' and educational leaders' treatment both of people and of knowledge. Having a voice, learners and staff members participate in deciding what is worth enquiry and effort. Finding they have a role to play beyond complying with given norms and repeating prepared information, they construct their own understanding and exercise their own authority.

How knowledge and people are treated

[At the level of lessons +
At the level of school organization and development]

Teachers'/Leaders' responsiveness
to pupils'/staff members' perceptions and choices,
seen in behaviour, distribution of authority, views

LOW   HIGH

TRANSPARENCY ◀ – – – – – – – – – – – – – – ▶ INTERACTIVITY

HIGH   LOW

Pupils'/Staff members' passivity and dependence,
seen in behaviour, scope of choices, views

An interactive classroom is more responsive to learners' perceptions and preferences than a transparent one. The equivalent is true for an interactive school or local authority in respect of staff members.

The shift from transparency to interactivity involves staff members and leaders giving up the appearance of being infallible. When leaders and staff members share responsibility for decisions, they are exposed to uncertainty, difficulty and error. Part of their learning has to be about flexibility and coping with setbacks. A primary school teacher saw it like this:

> *Helping the children understand their learning intentions means helping them learn how to learn. We are trying to enable our children to see it isn't about right and wrong, but about having a go. It's about confidence and talk and seeing themselves as learners. They can parrot what we've told them, but we want them to learn what learning really is. We are making progress. We have to keep referring to the 'We're learning ...', keep saying 'Wow, we now know ...', say to them 'Can you be the teacher?'*

A secondary school deputy headteacher approached whole-school and staff development in an equivalent way:

> *It's that notion of trust: they are the experts in their fields, their subjects, and so without their involvement and guidance in the process, where would your process lead? Staff not only leading, but initiating change. That's really important for staff to have the autonomy to feel they can bring those kinds of thoughts and ideas to the table, that they can direct the path that the research goes down ... That's how you keep initiatives like this a part of everyday practice.*

Helping to decide what to focus on, how to proceed, how to judge progress, and so on, has significant effects: psychological as well as social. A classroom's and institution's culture affects learners' or staff members' motivation and sense of themselves (cf. Dweck, 2000). It can also bring them into conflict with prevailing norms and regulations.

Some colleagues we worked with were sharply critical, for example, of a content-heavy and narrowly tested national curriculum, the absence of explicit criteria to guide pupils' test performance, and poor marking of end-of-key-stage test papers. Some expressed dismay that educational leaders set their sights no higher than transparency. Some were frustrated that colleagues could not see that the way professional and institutional development is carried out has a direct bearing on the kinds of learning that are promoted in lessons.

Helping to make important decisions

Here again are the ten things to be clear about in teaching and learning, referred to in Chapter 1 and shown as Appendix 2:

[1]   How do we work together?   = Ethos

[2]   What do we know about this topic?   = Prior knowledge
[3]   What are we trying to achieve?   = Intention
[4]   What might be interesting about this?   = Interest
[5]   How can we know how well we're doing?   = Criteria
[6]   How do we tackle it?   = Method
[7]   What can we do when we get stuck or
      go wrong?   = Resilience
[8]   What have we achieved?   = Achievement
[9]   How can we improve?   = Improvement
[10] How can we use what we learn?   = Application

The numbers can be used to analyse lesson observations, colleagues' reflections in interview or writing, and pupils' comments in interview and group discussion. Here are some examples.

This is a research team member's notes on a literacy lesson in an infant school's combined Year 1 and 2 class:

- The pupils organize themselves within a secure framework of routines and procedures (e.g. standing up to find their own talk partner to work with and resolving the problem of individuals left unattached). [1, 6, 7]
- The pupils express themselves in their own voice and by adopting other voices in order to explore information and ideas (e.g. through hotseating). [1, 4, 6]
- The pupils show how they feel about their progress/understanding/ confidence (e.g. by giving thumbs up, or thumbs sideways or thumbs down). [5, 7, 8]
- The pupils talk about how the lesson fits with the broader scheme of work (e.g. carrying on with work already begun, linking with details in other subjects . . .). [2, 3, 10]
- The pupils think for a while without putting their hand up to show they have an answer to a question. [1, 6, 7]
- The pupils talk to a partner to work out and share their ideas. [1, 4, 6, 7]
- The pupils list their rules for talking partners (e.g. they say: *Keep eye contact. Listen to them or you won't know. Don't talk over one another*). [1, 3, 5]
- The pupils list what they need to remember in their task, referring both to specific items (*Write the date. Carry on till the great fire of London is finished*) and to generic aspects (*Punctuation, capital letters. Use exciting words. Put your name on it. Use neat handwriting*). [3, 5]
- The pupils gauge their effort (Teacher: *How do you know you're trying your hardest?* Pupil: *We're quiet.* Teacher: *Yes, you've had your chance to*

talk, and now you're thinking and concentrating). [1, 5, 8, 10]
- The pupils' exercise books contain written feedback from the teacher relating explicitly to criteria for the task (*Great detail. Lots of information. Well punctuated*). [5, 8, 9]

Interactive teachers want learners to help in the planning of lessons and course activities. This junior school deputy headteacher saw scope for this, linking pupil voice with assessment for learning, while noting how too much change can disrupt progress:

> *One of the things that has come out of the ideas that the children had as to how we can make learning fun, things that we could implement, was the idea of the children being part of the planning for that topic, and actually it's something that we used to do. Pre-QCA. A lot of our planning was changed over for all the new stuff that came in, which was a real shame. But I was talking to my class and I said 'Well actually yes, we could tell you what our new topic is going to be after half term, and we could brainstorm all the things that you would like to find out about in that topic', and actually that is something we do anyway because we often do concept maps at the beginning to see what they know. Or we might fill in the KWL grid: what it is I* know, *what it is I* would *like to know, and then how I am going to find that out (*learn*). And a lot of our topic work is done through research and so the children can often lead that anyway. So that would be the next development.* [1, 2, 3, 4, 6, 7]

There were outstanding cases of pupils devising activities and assessments, as these secondary school pupils reported:

> *We had an active part in our curriculum and how we learn and what we learn. We changed mark schemes so it was easier for us to mark and for the class to understand. Instead of reading it and thinking 'Um, not sure what that means', we had a better understanding of what we had to achieve to get the grades.* [3, 5]

Mirroring this, it became more common for teachers to lead development in their own schools. And as a result of student voice work there were outstanding cases of learners making presentations to teachers and senior leaders. A newly qualified secondary school teacher (**NQT**) illustrated how the learning community project was influencing the culture of her school. She reported what she had learned from pupils who gave a presentation to the whole staff on a training day:

> *They said how AfL is used to give the students a voice in their lessons, speak about their own learning, and how to improve... It was really nice to know that it does matter to them... And to know they are supported by the senior staff...*

What I took from what the students had to say was how they use their prior knowledge, and how I use their progress to plan my lessons, and how I word my learning objectives... Especially for a discussion based lesson, if you've got that one question to keep coming back to, it does make it more succinct: 'So we're learning about this... We're going to talk about this...'. You can just ask that question again... I do think it makes the pupils feel that they're more involved, because if you ask them a question you're showing that you value their opinion, and not just standing at the front and saying 'This is what you're going to talk about today'. That's the important bit: to make them feel more involved. It's all about getting them from being passive to active which is interesting. [2, 3, 4, 6, 8, 9]

A good test of a lesson, topic or course is the proportion of time the learners spend in sustained, concentrated, worthwhile activity. We observed that this is greater in transparent classrooms than in prescriptive ones, greater in interactive classrooms than in transparent ones, and greatest when pupils set up and pursue their own activities.

Fascinating illustrations of this are seen in primary- and secondary-age schools which have developed 'learning logs'. These enable pupils to devise and carry out projects in their own time at home, as well as at school. Examples of lessons with interactive features are given in Appendix 7 and in quotations and lesson excerpts throughout. Examples of whole-school development are in Appendix 9.

4 'How do we work together?'

> **Fostering ETHOS: a sense of belonging**
> - Using groundrules
> - Helping one another and learning as partners
> - Taking responsibility and making choices
> - Using think-time
> - Being treated as an individual
> - Being open about not knowing, and being flexible
> - Teamwork in professional and whole-school development

This chapter covers important aspects of how pupils work with one another, assistants and teachers. The principles are seen also to apply to professional and whole-school development.

Using groundrules

At the beginning of the year, after a holiday, and when there has been some kind of crisis or breakdown in relationships, teachers lay down rules to govern behaviour in lessons. Some teachers do more than this though. They promote a proactive culture. This allows pupils to give their points of view and say how they want lessons to go. They share in decision-making about who does what. They agree clear procedures, so that everyone can have ways of dealing with problems that inevitably arise from time to time.

Explicit routines do more than set the scene for what is about to happen. They also give feedback on what is being achieved. A very effective way of doing this is circle time. Jenny Mosley (2000), with her team of consultants, has been an outstanding leader in this. Another method is to display posters outlining expectations and processes. The more involved pupils are in making and revising statements about conduct, the more likely they are to develop a healthy and considerate ethos.

The message that some teachers succeed in conveying is that what happens in lessons is more than the adults' concern. Lessons can be every class member's concern. All of this starts with clarity about expectations, and that means making criteria explicit.

Criteria are called 'golden rules' in some early years and primary-age settings. Their function is to help pupils learn how to regulate, reflect on and improve their behaviour. The focus can be on respect and kindness. This is about how teachers and assistants treat pupils, how pupils treat one another and their assistants and teachers.

Interactive teaching values dialogue. The onus can be on the learners to discuss and suggest solutions to problems in the group. A junior school teacher explained her experience of this:

> *In circle time we talked about problems felt when putting hands up for questions and answer sessions. Alternatives were discussed, and the pupils were in favour of using the whiteboards. We have also tried thumbs up, and standing up, red/green cards. We are clear the purpose of these experiments is to reduce the negative feelings. We now have a trend of using discussion and reflection to solve problems as a class.*

In interactive teaching pupils have more of a role than doing what they are told. They are encouraged to talk about what they are doing, what's going well, what isn't going well, and how things could be made better. This is very unlike the kind of teaching that demands 'Just do as I say', 'Work on your own in silence' or 'Make sure you get it right'. Junior school pupils expressed their appreciation of openness:

> *She explains what's happening and makes you feel glad. It's really really good. We feel comfortable. We all love this school.*

There are links here with other aspects of whole-school development which affect relationships, attitudes and behaviour. These include: citizenship; healthy schools; social and emotional aspects of learning (**SEAL**); personalization; and inclusion. What makes this a part of assessment for learning is the focus on criteria. (Chapter 8 covers the use of criteria in more detail.)

Talking about what kind of place pupils, teacher and assistant want the classroom to be helps everyone learn how to learn.

Reflection 4.1

Check how you and your pupils voice your expectations.

I make clear what I expect in these ways:

. . . .

. . . .

. . . .

My pupils make clear what they expect in these ways:

. . . .

. . . .

. . . .

Check how problems are aired and solutions found.

How do your pupils discuss ways of making lessons go well?

We discuss what's going well and how to improve lessons in these ways:

. . . .

. . . .

. . . .

. . . .

NEXT STEP

My pupils can be more involved in deciding and reviewing our groundrules by:

. . . .

. . . .

. . . .

Helping one another and learning as partners

Some teachers make a deliberate distinction between 'talk partners' and 'response partners'. Talk partners can mean working together to share ideas and help one another, for example, getting started or developing the work. Response partners (or critical friends, or peer assessors) can mean marking one another's work by referring to explicit criteria. The one is purely supportive, the other is constructively critical.

Talk partners can operate informally, pupils just turning to someone near them. But they can be set up more carefully, for example, the teacher deciding who will work with whom. Response partners are more likely to be arranged by the teacher, and guidance in the form of criteria needs to be prepared, with or without the pupils' input. The more of a say the pupils have in evolving these routines, the more interactive their experience and learning.

When pupils find they can do things, they begin to believe in themselves as capable learners. They are much more likely to do this if they help one another.

This is what some primary school teachers said about talk partners:

> *It gives them time to think and form ideas, using another child as a sounding board.*

> *We use it all the time. It allows for greater consideration of the problem.*

Learners can be asked to think about what makes helpful partnerships. They show themselves vary capable from an early age at analysing subtle properties and processes. This is what a first school class agreed with their teaching assistant and teacher as guidance for when they work as peer assessors:

- Be honest
- Say what's good/not so good
- Give reasons
- Ask/say why you did something/how you did it

The same pupils evaluated their experience of peer assessment:

> *Peer assessment helps you get more interesting ideas. . .*
> *Doing peer assessment helps you be a better writer by helping us work together. . .*
> *You get what other people think, not just what you think. . .*
> *Peer assessment helps you learn the success criteria. . .*
> *It helps you to really know what your target is.*

(This is explored further in Chapters 8, 11 and 12.)

Reflection 4.2

Think about how your pupils encourage and help one another.

My pupils have these ways of encouraging and helping one another:

. . . .

. . . .

. . . .

NEXT STEP

My pupils can encourage and help one another more effectively by:

. . . .

. . . .

. . . .

Taking responsibility and making choices

Interactive teachers see that, if learners are to work well together and get the best out of their activities, they have to take responsibility for their own behaviour and accept their part in maintaining the health of the group. Interactive teachers develop routines which give learners roles in lesson organization and decision-making. One way of doing this is to give learners specific choices about what they do and how they do it. Pupils become more committed when they opt into tasks and follow preferences.

A secondary school teacher reflected on how she had changed her approach:

> *I started thinking along the lines of 'Give pupils more control over their own learning', and I saw results in my classroom teaching.*

This junior school teacher explained how she and her colleagues offer a menu of choices at the end of the week:

Extended learning: it's something we do on Friday afternoon during the last half hour of school time... a chance to choose an activity from a varied menu outside of the normal curriculum offered by each teacher, and follow it for half a term. I am doing computer animation: you can see some examples on our website. Other activities are: junk percussion, paper maché, drama, model gardens, crochet, weaving. One of the Year 6 boys came in to show me his woven 'Mexican eyes' this morning!

Personal responsibility is a key, as a secondary school teacher commented:

It's about keeping up a sense of pace, not getting bogged down, and moving them forward so that they're enjoying what they're doing and learning, and taking responsibility for their learning, rather than it being spoon-fed to them...

The significant point is that the pupils are helped to be aware of and explicit about how they work. As this secondary school pupil said:

You need to learn how to do group work, and you need to know how to work independently as well.

This entails knowing how to deal with difficulties and mistakes (which Chapter 10 explores in more detail). A junior school deputy headteacher spoke about it in these terms:

There is an issue of what can be called learned helplessness. In my lower maths set I have moved the pupils so that they no longer sit in groups: all sit together and have to think for themselves. We emphasize 'We are your helpers', not 'We are going to do it for you; you must do what you need to do.' This was good for some, but others felt they were not contained. We are trying to help them see you can't just sit there. We have been timing how long it takes for them to organize themselves. We are working out how to support the pupils rather than letting them think there is always someone there to tell them what to do. We are always trying to find more options: as teachers, and for the pupils to have more options too. We are using the children more.

Learners can be asked to prepare their own projects along simple lines. They can decide, for example:

- What am I aiming to achieve?
- What help do I need?
- How do I want my work to be assessed?

Reflection 4.3

Check how you pass responsibility and ownership to your pupils.

I enable my pupils to take responsibility for and ownership of their activities in these ways:

. . . .

. . . .

. . . .

NEXT STEP

My pupils can have more initiative by:

. . . .

. . . .

. . . .

Using think-time

A key message is that thinking is valued. One of the main areas for experiment in AfL is giving pupils 'think time' or 'wait time'. This does not obviously relate to assessment, and is more of a generic teaching strategy: to give learners prompts and support to reflect. There are many ways of doing this. For example, 'I want you to think for a minute (or ten seconds, or half a minute. . .) about this question, and then I'll ask some of you what you think' or 'Think about your ideas, then turn to your partner and share them with one another, before we all get back together and hear what you've all come up with.'

A junior school deputy headteacher reflected on how far she had come, and on how far she and her colleagues still had to go, towards having all the pupils engaged in questioning and answering:

> When I really think about it, I say 'Think for two minutes'. It is difficult for those who are keen to answer, and I don't want to dampen their enthusiasm. It is difficult to keep everyone involved and avoiding the weaker pupils feeling threatened. The key is in giving the pupils the skills, and we have a way to go on this. Our classroom observation and monitoring can focus on this.

This junior school teacher knew the development was not easy:

> *First they were shocked that I waited before asking someone to answer, when I said no hands up. It took nearly a term to get out of the habit of putting hands up. I had to get them out of thinking answers are right or wrong. I say I don't know the answer sometimes, so they see me as someone who needs to think and learn.*

But these junior school pupils were reaping the benefits:

> *It's good when you get to talk to a partner about a question because you can share your ideas and come up with a better answer.*

> *When you can't put your hands up everybody has to think of an answer, and the teacher might ask you.*

> *She gives us two minutes to decide. She's a good teacher, the best I've ever had. Sometimes it's no hands up and lucky dip. Sometimes people have their hand up and are not picked. She can pick a shy one to help them be not so shy. She always listens to us.*

This infant school teacher saw signs of progress:

> *The quality of questions asked by teachers in lessons has improved. Previously we answered our own questions without realizing it. Now, with the consistent use of wait time, the children answer.*

And these primary school pupils observed:

> *Wait time makes us think and gives us more confidence as we get the answer right.*

> *You don't know who she is going to pick so you work out the answer.*

> *We don't put our hands up; you have to think about it. This is so that everybody has time to think, and you have to have an answer in case you are asked. If there is a difficult question, the teacher will just give time to think about an answer which can be helpful.*

Questions can prompt learners to explain their thinking. We found that many of the teachers we worked with were conscious of wanting to develop in their pupils the capacity to share their thinking with others. Where possible, therefore, they tried to avoid giving responses that suggest there are hard-and-fast right or wrong answers. This leads to the asking of more open than closed questions. And it means a climate of discussion has to be fostered that encourages courage and risk-taking. 'No put-downs' is the rule. These teachers praised their pupils for trying hard to express difficult ideas and how they arrived at them.

Reflection 4.4

Have a critical look at questioning in your lessons.

Who asks questions? How many pupils really think about the questions? How do you help them learn about asking and answering questions?

Questions are usually posed in these formats:

. . . .

. . . .

. . . .

NEXT STEP

My pupils can learn more about how to answer questions by:

. . . .

. . . .

. . . .

Being treated as an individual

Receiving one-to-one attention is something pupils appreciate more than anything else. Planning and lesson organization can avoid long sequences of whole-class teaching, and give time and space to individuals and small groups. Email communication between teachers and learners is also an exciting development in some schools.

But school is an impersonal experience for some pupils. Teachers have to make a deliberate effort to help pupils feel they are not lost in the crowd. A primary school pupil put it like this:

The teacher talks to you and tells you if there are things that you could do better. It helps when the teacher talks to you by yourself. Working in small groups with the teacher is also good.

Some teachers find ways of opening up dialogue, sometimes spoken, sometimes written, between their pupils and themselves. This secondary school teacher gave a presentation to colleagues on a training day:

I ask the pupils from time to time to write what they want in a special notebook about how their work in English is going. I don't mark what they write, but speak when possible to individuals about what they write. I use this experience to learn about what the students find useful, what they find difficult, what they find enjoyable... They are encouraged to be honest and to see it as a way of helping me teach as well as I can. Sometimes I read the books out of lesson time, sometimes in lessons. Sometimes the students read their latest entry aloud in class...

She went on to answer her colleagues' questions:

Q: *Have you lost teaching time as a result?*
A: *No, not really. We did it occasionally, sometimes instead of the conventional plenary.*
Q: *Did you always tell them when to write something in the notebook, or did they choose?*
A: *Both.*
Q: *Have they improved more rapidly?*
A: *Of course, it's hard to tell what would have happened if I hadn't done this. But they have made strong progress, and it's helped me realize that. It's definitely made them more reflective.*
Q: *Have you any tips, and will you be doing it with other students and year groups?*
A: *Think about the practicalities of the class, when to fit it in, for example, and the management of the books. I will be doing this with all my groups now.*

And her pupils told me about their notebooks:

I think they're good! To recap what we have learned and what we didn't understand too!

It gave us a chance to say something back.

It's been helpful because I can look back and see what I have learnt in other lessons.

I think the notebooks are great, all years should have them up to Year 11 and then they could use them for GCSEs. I think it would help a lot.

One of the most effective ways of signalling that the individual counts is to ask what s/he thinks and feels, and to take the answers seriously. Pupils learn whether or not teachers, assistants and their peers can be trusted not to make fun of them or belittle them, but accept and respect them for being who they are.

Reflection 4.5

Consider how your pupils come to feel they count as individuals.

My pupils get personal attention and feel they have a voice, when:

. . . .

. . . .

. . . .

. . . .

NEXT STEP

My pupils can feel they matter and are taken seriously more by:

. . . .

. . . .

. . . .

Being open about not knowing, and being flexible

Interactive teachers develop flexibility in their responses and methods. They tend not to stick rigidly to systems, but change their ways of handling issues that arise. They present themselves as learners alongside their pupils.

Some teachers are skilled at 'making deliberate mistakes' and 'needing help', so skilled that their pupils aren't aware they're being asked to show how things should be done. These junior school pupils, for example, spoke about their teacher's 'difficulties' which they kindly help her overcome:

We help her be organized. . .
We don't mind her losing things. . .
She's got lots of things to help us. . .
Like the jotter: we can put anything in it. . .
Like if someone says a good word, we can jot it down. . .
We can use any way to help. . .
She gave us a test to help her to see what subject we like best and what to improve on. This could be a big thing. I think it'll do well and we'll benefit. . .
It's nice she considers our opinion and how we feel.

Outstanding teachers don't have all the answers. These junior school teachers are open about the fact that they are continually evolving their teaching methods to suit their pupils:

We have learning journals, started before Easter. What pupils have told me, for example, about my marking, has changed my approach.

I have been made to reflect on myself as a teacher. When I began, I just marked things right or wrong. Now I question my teaching, fine tune it, and think about why I am doing what I am doing.

This secondary school teacher lets pupils in on the fact that she is trying to find the best possible methods for them:

Within the school there are potentially two schools of thought. One, that it's the teacher's knowledge, but you don't share it with them. And there's the other approach, where you actually tell them why you're doing it, because that's how they learn and that's how the brain works. Well, I'm in that camp. That's why I always explain to them why I'm seating them boy-girl, why I'm giving them a little break, how long I think they ought to be able to concentrate for. . . why they're doing learning logs. . . I suppose it's maybe that you keep more control, if you don't tell them why you're doing something.

Interactive teachers ask their pupils about the success or otherwise of activities and strategies. They let their pupils in on the effort of trying to get the most out of what they do. So they ask 'How well did that approach work for you? How can we make it work better?'

Reflection 4.6

Consider how you show you need your pupils' help.

My pupils see I need their help, when:

. . . .

. . . .

. . . .

NEXT STEP

My pupils can develop an even better partnership with me by:

. . . .

. . . .

. . . .

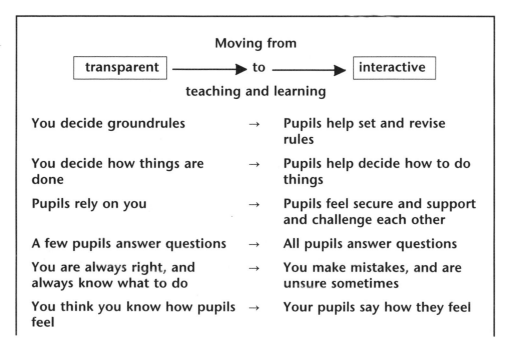

Moving from

| transparent | ——→ to ——→ | interactive |

teaching and learning

You decide groundrules	→	Pupils help set and revise rules
You decide how things are done	→	Pupils help decide how to do things
Pupils rely on you	→	Pupils feel secure and support and challenge each other
A few pupils answer questions	→	All pupils answer questions
You are always right, and always know what to do	→	You make mistakes, and are unsure sometimes
You think you know how pupils feel	→	Your pupils say how they feel

Individuals are overlooked	→	Everyone has attention and a voice
There is one-way, top-down communication between staff members and leaders	→	You work as teams and collectively

Teamwork in professional and whole-school development

Interactive teaching makes serious demands on clarity of thinking and resourcefulness. This is why working with other colleagues is so important: to share planning and teaching experiences, to encourage one another and problem solve together. It takes proactive leadership to guide and support this kind of development.

These secondary school teachers illustrate how important it is for there to be cohesion between staff members and with their leaders:

> *I need behind me a senior management team who are all saying the same thing... I need to know that if I meet* [the headteacher's] *standards and work within her boundaries, and it goes funny, she will be on my side. It doesn't mean you don't make mistakes, but it means that, when you do make mistakes, it's dealt with in a nice, sympathetic way. A good senior management team is worth much more than any amount of money you could throw at me for books. If I was told you could have an unsupportive deputy head and two grand for books, I'd choose a good deputy head any day. In terms of the classroom, I find that the vast majority of the work on helping children orientate themselves has already been done by somebody else. You have a senior management team that has standards. You have pastoral team that support you, that know about what subjects they do. You have tutors who talk to their pupils and do targets... So the key question is 'Who else's job do I have to do as well as mine?' No, just mine.*

> *We're not islands. We do work in a complex network of not just me in my classroom, but me in my department and in my school.*

> *What's become interesting is that by doing these AfL strategies it has increased the amount of professional dialogue within the school, between teachers. There's been a whole culture of expertise sharing.*

And this secondary school teacher illustrates how important cooperation is within subject, curriculum or year teams:

We are generally a very cohesive department. We meet fortnightly and we're always open to new ideas. And one of the things we do at our meetings, once a half term, is to talk about something that we've done recently that's gone well. So we get an opportunity to see it, to share it, to talk about it, to think about why that might have worked, and to go away and try it. Over the course of a year we all do this once. It's our own INSET if you like. Some of those things have then become embedded in our practice throughout the department, but others are peculiar to individuals, which is fine. We have certain things that we all agree we will do at certain points, but beyond that it's all down to individual preference and taste as to how we deliver. We are not robots or machines... The one that a colleague did last night was 'I've been trying to get my head around target-setting, so this is what I've done. What do you think?' And she brought a pile of exercise books, talked us through the piece of work... 'What I've asked the children to do is... Problem I'm having is...' And we talked it through. Because that is something we're trying to get pupils to do: to feed forward. We're trying to get them to think of where they've come from, where they've got to go next. They tend to be too woolly, if you don't train them, they tend to write 'Got to do better' which is rubbish: we want smart targets really. We are trying to teach them to think in small achievable realistic terms in **MFL** [modern foreign languages], *and that's what she was talking about last night.*

Reflection 4.7

Identify the support you get from other colleagues and the school's leadership.

I have these ways of giving feedback on the support I get from colleagues and the leadership:

. . . .

. . . .

. . . .

Consider how colleagues share experiences and ideas.

We have these ways of documenting our teamwork and collaboration:

. . . .

. . . .

. . . .

NEXT STEP

In the next cycle of evaluation and development planning, we can highlight the quality of leadership and colleagues' sharing of experiences and ideas by:

. . . .

. . . .

. . . .

See Chapter 14 about professional and institutional development, and Appendix 9 for examples.

5 'What do we know about this topic?'

Building on PRIOR KNOWLEDGE: using what we know

- Recapping and seeing learning grow
- Mind-mapping and using learning walls/mats
- Taking stock to see the way forward

This chapter covers ways in which what learners already know can launch the next steps in their learning. The same principles are applied to professional and whole-school development.

Recapping and seeing learning grow

A common practice, designed to elicit and revise knowledge and skills, is teacher-led question-and-answer. Questions can be aimed at summing up key ideas in recent work. They can round off a lesson with conclusions. They can also refer to out-of-school experience and other curriculum subjects, as well as previous lessons.

On the one hand, this helps teachers appreciate pupils' present capability. The better teachers understand their pupils, the better they can help them learn. A secondary school teacher put it like this:

You can't plan for children you don't know.

On the other hand, looking back over what they have learned helps pupils see patterns and structures in their knowledge and skills. When learners express what they know, or show what they can do, they benefit cognitively *and* affectively: getting a morale boost as well as an opportunity to rehearse and reinforce capability. Their confidence grows that they can learn more.

When teachers are aware of this, they make their recapping questions focus on connections and reasoning, rather than isolated and random pieces of information. They help their pupils realize how well they are doing and how to prepare for the next challenge. This does not mean that gaps, deficits and misunderstandings cannot be used to promote learning (see Chapters 10 and

12), but it shifts the emphasis onto positive achievement as a basis for further effort.

Continuity between lessons promotes progression in learning. Consolidation involves maintaining interest as well as momentum and direction. This secondary school teacher explained:

> *To me there is an unbroken link between one lesson and the next: that is the key. I'm very prepared to do something at the beginning of a lesson which is a repeat of the last one. I think you need to consolidate a lot more than people think. In a way we try always to do too much. It's like the analogy with the bird of prey: I keep thinking about it. Even the most avaricious bird of prey will stop eating if force-fed.*

Learners as well as teachers benefit from knowing 'where they are' before they can confidently know how they might progress. As these comments explain:

> Infant school teacher: *It is all about getting pupils to understand where they are now and how to get where they want to be.*

> Primary school teacher: *Children are now more aware of the big picture: what do we know already, and what are we going to learn about?*

Teachers help their pupils step back or go over something again. Pupils register how teachers feel things are going. Teachers and pupils pick up information all the time from one another – about what they grasp and what they are struggling with; about what they are pleased and displeased by. Teachers and pupils provide this dynamic feedback both inadvertently and deliberately in their body language, as well as in what they say. This can highlight what progress has been secured and where attention is now needed.

A secondary school teacher illustrated this dynamic process:

> *I focus on what it is I want the pupils to know, and what it is I want them to retain. I have to bear in mind 'Did they grasp it easily the previous lesson?', in which case 'Can I afford to take more of a leap?' Or 'Were we going round in small circles?' and I need to find a way out of that. Or to reinforce something that I consider to be really important, and that I think they really need to know, I need to find a new way of tackling it. It comes through things they've said, things we've done in the lesson, their books: there's a whole host of kinds of information that inform that judgement as to what we're going to do next.*

A colleague in the same school spoke similarly about how formative assessment shapes planning:

You're assessing if that went well, if that was successful. You're kind of implicitly doing that as you're going. And so you're thinking 'What do I need to pick up on in the next lesson? Would I do that the same way next time? Would I have time to do it the same way? Or do I need to move on to something else?' And if it didn't work, what if certain people were disruptive or difficult, weren't accessing it, you're thinking 'Do I need to do it differently next time? Do I need to re-visit that? How do I need to help those few who didn't grasp that?'... It's like it's a rolling story, and you don't necessarily know which chapter you're going to get to at the end of the lesson, do you?... Sometimes I know, but not always. It's often like a map: you could go that way, or you can go that way as well.

The interesting thing is that this is an interactive process: teachers *and* learners give and receive feedback. The question is: how well do they use the information?

Reflection 5.1

Think about how you and your pupils find out where they are up to in their learning.

My pupils show what they already know and can do in these ways:

. . . .

. . . .

. . . .

NEXT STEP

We can build on my pupils' existing knowledge and skills more effectively by:

. . . .

. . . .

. . . .

Mind-mapping and using learning walls/mats

Interactive teachers try different ways of enabling their pupils to check and build on what they know for themselves. Transparent teaching has pupils display what they know on noticeboards and walls, on paper or 'mats' on their desks. Interactive teaching enables pupils to use representations of what they are learning to help them make decisions about its quality and where to take it next.

A sign that transparency is moving toward interactivity is teachers involving learners in making mind-maps, whereby the pupils plot what they already know and suggest questions and topics they would like to explore. A junior school teacher gave an example:

> *Where a concept map was developed with children before a unit of work on World War Two, it was amazing how much they already knew.*

And a primary school teacher reflected on what this strategy was achieving:

> *Mind-mapping has 'opened a door' which might provide the opportunity for children to be involved in writing learning intentions.*

An extended version of this is the display of all kinds of materials relating to the pupils' work: plans, questions, ideas, examples of work, suggestions, comments, criteria, celebrations... These go by various names, such as learning or working walls or mats. They can give an individual focus or reinforce the pupils' understanding that they are all working and learning together. And it provides excellent opportunities for the pupils to pose their own questions.

With the modern curriculum there is a tendency for teachers and assistants to feel they have too much ground to cover and no time for opening discussion out to questions that enrich learning, questions that the learners have themselves. So it is helpful to have certain occasions and forums for learners to say what is puzzling and intriguing. Mind-maps and learning walls are ideal spaces for this.

A secondary school teacher described how she uses what her pupils know and what they don't know to plan progressive sequences of learning activities:

> *We've just started an introduction to the media and I stripped it right down to the basics, telling them that these things that they come across every day are 'the media'. That was the moment that I realized that some of them had an idea of this already, but the majority of them thought that the media was newspapers. So that was quite useful to then be able to move onto the next lesson and take*

out the different type of media products, how it works, different forms of media, all that sort of thing. So I could structure that lesson to give them the key terminology before we go into more detail. So they help me understand what they need. Which I much prefer, because I hate that moment, which I obviously did a lot in my training year, when you realize that they're staring at you and they want to understand what you're saying, but they've not got it. So I've found that this way is about the modelling and the stepping stones, so you can know they're with you and interacting with you... I tend to start off with mind-mapping, so that they can put down all their ideas. That then comes back to a group feedback, and then you can see where the holes are in their knowledge, and you can start to show them the connections. And then I find that if they're doing paired work or in groups, they can focus on one point from each mind-map section. So the first lesson in a unit I try to make quite discussion based, so that there's a lot of chance for them to ask questions of each other, to me, and that works. It helps build a relationship. They see that they're all pulling together.

Reflection 5.2

Check how your pupils help decide what questions to explore and what challenges to take on.

My pupils have these ways of setting the agenda:

. . . .

. . . .

. . . .

NEXT STEP

My pupils can be more involved in deciding how to take their learning forward by:

. . . .

. . . .

. . . .

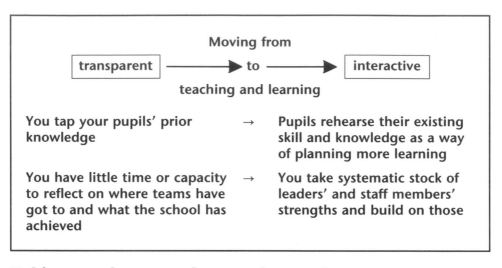

Taking stock to see the way forward

What is true for pupils' learning in lessons is true also for professionals' development and whole-school improvement.

Teachers with experience of action research try to avoid beginning initiatives as though they had never before thought about teaching and learning. They take fresh ideas and renewed commitment forward on the basis of what they have already achieved individually, in their teams and across the school. This infant school teacher saw it like this:

> The project has meant stepping back and thinking about what we are doing. It is important not to change too much, and to make alterations step by step. It is also important not to change things that already work well.

One of the most effective ways of improving teaching and learning is to identify what is successful and to concentrate on bringing everyone's performance up toward that level. Here is an example of a junior school staff consolidating their progress in AfL. They used a staff meeting to agree these statements as a way of maintaining and strengthening consistency across the school:

> We use a variety of methods and media to communicate our learning intentions and success criteria in order to create a shared understanding amongst our pupils:
> - written/displayed on the board
> - shown by modelling and explained
> - by mnemonic
> - using first-hand experience or shown virtually.

We make varied use of our learning intentions and success criteria in assessment:

- *pupils' self assessment*
- *pupils' peer assessment*
- *using pupils' work as a model*
- *in spoken and written assessment*
- *asking pupils to apply their learning in an extended example*
- *giving red herrings for the pupils to identify*
- *enabling/asking pupils to transfer their learning across subjects*
- *asking pupils to use their learning in problem contexts.*

We expect that anyone observing our lessons will see a range of features of good practice in relation to how we use learning intentions and success criteria:

- *activities differentiated, e.g. into what pupils must, should, could achieve*
- *taking account of pupils' different learning styles in the ways we share learning intentions and success criteria*
- *asking pupils to apply their understanding in plenary questions*
- *constructive marking, including peer marking and self assessment*
- *clear signs of pupils making progress*
- *clear signs that pupils enjoy their work, feel it is worthwhile, feel good about themselves, and can say what they have done well*
- *giving pupils opportunities to interact with learning intentions and success criteria, to own them.*

Appraising current performance can be harsh, but, with a determination to affirm areas of strength, challenges can be constructive and realistic. Here is a secondary school's senior leader summarizing where his school is up to, launching the next phase of development in good faith and confidence:

View of AfL in the school
AfL is a foundation block of good teaching and good lessons. It involves establishing a baseline in the pupils' understanding. The format for schemes of work should ensure that AfL is built in, but this cannot yet be claimed with confidence across the board. Too many teachers run lessons by teaching content and ignoring where the pupils are. There have been improvements in summative assessment and the use of that. Performance management is not yet consistently linked to developments in the area of assessment. The subject leaders' knowledge is key.

Areas of strength or interest
Art, dance and drama are areas of high success in the school.

By the end of Year 11 pupils should have experienced...
Being equipped for the world where they see the point of their activities. It is a whole-person thing. It has a spiritual dimension, related to dealing with uncertainty. It involves expecting to know their success criteria and how to achieve them.

Barriers to realizing the full benefits of AfL
*A lack of experienced teachers. The school has 25 non-qualified or very recently qualified teachers (**GTP** and NQTs). Able teachers take on responsibilities that take them out of the classroom, but we need our good teachers to teach.*

What helps?
Having the staff. Time for planning. AfL needs to be developed over time, refreshed, and for the staff to be challenged to make it happen. This month sees a training day on accelerated learning.

Conclusion
*This is a highly inspected school with recruitment problems and, in the recent past, school closures because of under-staffing. A calendar for summative assessment is in place; how should this now take account of AfL? An issue raised by the recent **HMI** visit concerned the students' passivity: how can they become more involved and active?*

Reflection 5.3

What are the strengths and weaknesses of your present policy and practice in AfL?

How do you know? Whose views are represented?

Where is an overview given? Who has access to that?

We have these ways of charting and evaluating our formative assessment policy and practice:

. . . .

. . . .

. . . .

Consider how you and your colleagues avoid the pressure of having always to move on and cover what other people seem to say has to be done.

We have these ways of taking control of our own development
and building on what we do well:

. . . .

. . . .

. . . .

NEXT STEP

We can more effectively consolidate our strengths and successes
by:

. . . .

. . . .

. . . .

6 'What are we trying to achieve?'

Working on INTENTION: having a purpose and trying

- Planning for learning and using targets
- Involving pupils in planning
- Learning how to learn
- Taking charge of professional and whole-school development

This chapter covers ways of preparing for learning by making intentions explicit. The last section carries the same principles over to professional and whole-school development.

Planning for learning and using targets

Defining learning objectives for lessons and topics is a cornerstone of formative assessment. Objectives can lay out the broad territory to be covered. They can also break complex actions down into manageable steps, break complicated matters into digestible chunks. They motivate by offering the prospect of success. There is no hard and fast rule for how objectives work. The point is that understanding their objectives focuses learners.

Transparent teaching communicates objectives to the pupils. As an infant school teacher said:

> *Children now know what it is they are doing, whereas before it was a 'secret'.*

An important aspect of this is to highlight the *learning*. 'What are you learning? What have you learned?' are under-used questions in some classrooms.

Trying to be clear about the learning, as opposed to the doing, is demanding. An infant school deputy headteacher admitted that it takes concentration to make this shift in thinking and practice:

> *I have learnt to look first at what it is I want the children to learn, rather than what I want them to do.*

To impose an orthodoxy is unhelpful, but it helps to share what works. A primary school teacher noted how a whole-school approach to documentation supported a better focus:

> *Planning sheets have been modified to separate the learning intention from the context, and a column has been incorporated for the inclusion of success criteria.*

An infant school teacher described her school's way of doing this:

> *We have small 'I am learning to. . .' stickers that go on the pupils' work to guide them, to help them check how they're doing, and show what they've achieved.*

Teachers who have developed such routines are confident of the benefits:

> Primary school teacher: *There is now a more explicit focus on the learning. Children are able to be more independent. There is less time spent waiting for them to get on with tasks. They know what they have to do and get on with it straight away. Lower ability children are much clearer about what they have to do.*

A primary school pupil appreciated the new emphasis:

> *It helps me to understand what I am supposed to do.*

It is also important that teaching assistants are in the picture, as these colleagues described:

> Infant school teacher: *The new format for learning objectives is easier to share with the teaching assistant. It is clear to her what the children are to gain from the work.*

> Primary school teacher: **TAs** (teaching assistants) *are clearer about what the children are trying to achieve.*

Clarifying objectives involves prioritizing. Important decisions have to be made, not only about what the main focus is, but about what becomes peripheral or optional and what can be left out. This infant school teacher explained:

> *Curriculum content may well need to be trimmed to allow for better quality learning, consolidation and follow-up work.*

This secondary school teacher similarly recognized how planning had to be more selective:

> *At Key Stage 4 it's unremittingly content-based. . . One of the things I make sure I do is make a list of the things I think I don't need to touch on, or I can leave out, or they can draw their own conclusions about: things I plan to cut out, so I can use the space for doing things with history. I don't want to deliver a sackful of potatoes; I want to try some recipes.*

One of the strongest implications of assessment for learning is that planning has not to be rigid but adjust to the learners' responses. Intentions have to change in the light of experience. These two infant school deputy headteachers analysed what the difference meant to them and their pupils:

> *I am now more flexible with my planning. If the learning intention has not been achieved, I adjust the planning to allow more time rather than moving on. This is much better practice in terms of pupil learning.*
>
> *Flexibility is essential: teachers taking decisions about what is in the best interest of the pupils.*

Individual learners and groups can have differentiated objectives. Some teachers specify which objectives *everyone must* tackle, which *most should* tackle, and which *some could* tackle. This is part of being flexible in defining lesson objectives for classes and groups and setting targets for individuals.

Most teachers speak about 'objectives' for lessons and 'targets' for individuals. For the whole school, 'targets' are statistically modelled constructs, used in the belief that they will generate aspiration and commitment and assist self-evaluation and public accountability. Perhaps the commonest problem with all of them is that they lose focus and relevance as time goes by. Hence the importance of being prepared to revise intentions (see Blanchard, 2002).

Trying to make targets motivating and productive is a challenge, requiring evaluation and adaptation. This is illustrated by the infant school teachers and assistants who agreed this statement at a staff meeting:

- *We share our experience of using targets and understand that we can learn from one another, because there is no single method that will guarantee success with all our pupils in all circumstances.*
- *We use targets to help our pupils understand what they are learning.*
- *We use targets to promote, focus and celebrate success for all our pupils.*
- *We use targets to contribute to our pupils' sense of security and confidence.*
- *We are working towards as much consistency in our practice as we can,*

without stifling our individuality and without neglecting the specific characters and contexts of our classes.

- *We refer to and adapt material that comes from advisory and statutory authorities.*
- *We use targets that are the priorities for learning in a lesson or sequence of lessons: there may be as few as one target, and we understand that more learning may occur than is expressed by the targets.*
- *Where possible we enable our pupils to engage with their targets in more than one medium and in multi-sensory ways.*
- *We frame targets in language that should be accessible to the pupils, sometimes using visual cues or icons.*
- *One of the possible functions of displaying targets for everyone to see is to show progression in learning.*
- *Targets displayed on the wall can set a kind of headline that unites the class in a common purpose and sense of identity.*
- *Targets displayed on the wall do not have pupils' names attached, unless we are sure that this does not demoralize the pupils or set up unhealthy comparisons.*
- *Targets for groups on tables have pupils' names and tend to be more personalized than wall-displayed targets.*
- *Individual pupils' targets may also be used.*
- *Our regular and formative use of targets with our pupils may lead us to review the need for some formal testing at the end of topics or terms.*
- *Sometimes our use of targets involves signalling success in a specific instance: recording these (e.g. in a checklist) gives a scan of a pupil's performance and can be shared with them.*
- *Sometimes our use of targets involves making as reliable a judgement as possible about the stage and level of capability pupils have reached: recording these goes towards Teacher Assessments and reports.*

Teachers and learners sometimes treat criteria as objectives. The two seem to overlap, but it can help to separate them. An objective effectively answers the question 'What are we trying to achieve?' A criterion effectively answers the question 'How do we know how well we're doing?' But if on occasion the distinction is blurred, it should not be a concern. What matters is not 'getting it right' in any theoretical sense. What matters is finding what helps your pupils learn effectively, and this can vary from group to group and from topic to topic.

Reflection 6.1

Sum up the key learning points for today's lesson/s.

Sum up the key learning points for one of your current topics / units.

I have these ways of making clear what I aim to teach:

. . . .

. . . .

. . . .

Share with colleagues ways of planning flexibly so that assessment can be used to inform next steps.

We have these ways of using assessment to change our planning:

. . . .

. . . .

. . . .

Examine how targets help your pupils learn.

My pupils benefit from using targets in these ways:

. . . .

. . . .

. . . .

NEXT STEP

We can develop our use of objectives and targets by:

. . . .

. . . .

. . . .

Involving pupils in planning

Objectives do not have always to be stated at the beginning. Sometimes it is more interesting to ask questions about what is being learned as activities develop. It can be very productive for the pupils to deduce what they have been learning from what they are doing. This infant school pupil confidently answered a researcher's questions:

> *What are you doing?*
>   *Making puppets.*
> *What are you learning?*
>   *How to write instructions.*

What turns transparent teaching into interactive teaching and learning is pupils having a voice in planning their activities. This infant school deputy headteacher, for example, described her school's process of development:

> *We tended to go from the learning intention to the activity in our planning. In writing it down we were not always clear, but in class we were often explicit to the children about what was needed. Now after Shirley Clarke's session, we use the pupils to repeat back more. It's a way of checking, giving them, or modelling, expectations. When we introduce something new, we model the steps. Sometimes I don't do this, and things go wrong. Explaining and modelling and going through are the best way...*
>
> *I've been speaking it, and only twice written it up so far. The thing is to do it* [i.e. write up intentions and criteria] *with the children, not for them. Ownership is the key. I am pleased with this so far.*

This secondary school teacher gives her pupils a role in deciding the purpose and focus for their work:

> *They set their own targets, having looked at comments that myself or each other have written. I don't feel I'm getting this from the pupils at the moment, but I am aiming that, by the time they get to Years 10 and 11, they will be able to identify that a lot of their own learning is their responsibility.*

A group of primary school teachers were developing their version of this:

> *We aim to develop 'the big picture': an overview of a term's work with questions that will generate learning intentions. This is shared with the pupils and displayed in the classroom. The pupils raise their own additional questions, which provide opportunities for research. When they finish a question area, pupils have a traffic light to show how they think they have done.*

Their conclusion was that:

> *The children need to be involved in the planning of their new learning.*

The pay-off is increased ownership and commitment, as this primary school pupil put it:

> *I've got to get it right because I suggested it!*

But not everything goes smoothly. This special school deputy headteacher described a process taking several months:

> *At first the development did not go well. Pupils were asked to choose learning objectives. There were too many, with too many possible variables for staff to respond to, and with too superficial an engagement by the pupils in them. They were onto their next choice and the next learning objective (**LO**) before they had really got to grips with the first choice. Staff were trying to keep up the quality of teaching that had been established, with good links between activities and pupils' individual education plans (**IEP**s), but staff were confused, and the pupils did not fully understand what they were choosing between, or why they were choosing. Part of the struggle has been for staff to trust the pupils' decisions and to take confidence in the quality of outcomes when pupils invest time and effort in making their choices.*
>
> *So the scheme of work has been retained and continues to be tweaked, because it works. But pupils are not asked to choose learning objectives. They choose from a selection of methods or ways of tackling learning objectives. E.g. LO 'Learn that humans have bodies with similar parts' leads to a choice of activities, (a) Look at the human body, (b) Find out how we move, (c) Find out who has same colour eyes as you, (d) Find out who has same colour hair as you; and each of those has a wide range of possibilities for pupils to negotiate choices, e.g. in terms of sensory input and media (internet, person-to-person enquiry, visit, pictures...), site, co-working, support, and so on.*
>
> *It is as though the staff have developed their definition of and responsibility for the learning track they want pupils to progress along, but they have accepted the challenge of inviting and enabling the pupils to make choices and decisions about how to proceed along the track: this affects pace and selection of context.*

Interactive teaching is a real challenge, as shown by this secondary school teacher's reflections:

> *In some ways I like the idea of it, but... it's almost a case of I'm not brave enough to try it just yet, until I feel I'm at a position where the group will be*

able to respond to it. . . I just feel, if you start shifting the ground and moving the goalposts, the pupils start to think 'Well, actually I'm not sure now what you do want of me', and that's why I'm a little bit apprehensive. . . . On the other hand you don't want it to stagnate. It's definitely something I've thought about since our last INSET, because I do wonder sometimes how you could prevent them becoming bored with the system. It's tricky: striking the balance. . . Maybe getting them to think of one question that you could ask to check: then you've got your question as your learning objective. Then I haven't given them anything. That would work: getting them to ask the question, a question that sums up to check 'whether you've understood what we've done so far.' That would then be a meaningful question, wouldn't it?. . . So along with all of their ordinary plenaries where you look back at what you've done that lesson, you've got something that's bigger, that's over-riding. . . You do want them to be aware of the fact that there is more to do to promote the idea of independent learning.

Committed and creative teachers strive to develop cooperation, critical reflectiveness, flexibility, and a shared focus on developing learners' autonomy as far as they can. A secondary school teacher reported on a presentation which pupils gave to staff during an INSET day about the lesson observations they had done:

They took notes on everything, how teachers use learning objectives, how pupils are treated, how routines are set up: what makes an ideal lesson from a pupil's point of view. Some of it was 'Yes, we guessed you'd like that', but parts of it were really interesting to hear them say 'If my homework and my learning objectives aren't interesting, I don't want to know'. Sometimes you wonder if they do pay any attention to their learning objectives. Well they do.

This kind of pupil participation in analysing and developing teaching methods and topics was one of the most impressive features of the project. It was instructive and rewarding for teachers and learners alike.

Reflection 6.2

Consider how you currently involve your pupils in giving their activities purpose and direction.

My pupils have these ways of helping to set objectives and targets:

. . . .

. . . .

. . . .

Consider ways of extending your pupils' decision-making about what they aim for.

NEXT STEP

My pupils can play more of a part in planning activities by:

. . . .

. . . .

. . . .

Learning how to learn

Setting objectives involves analysing what tasks and challenges require. Interactive teaching opens up that process to the learners, helping them to learn how to backtrack from what they are asked to do, or want to do, and break it down into the necessary components.

Focusing attention on objectives can promote awareness of learning beyond subject content and bring status to generic, cross-curricular, social and personal aspects of learning. A junior school deputy headteacher saw that a step in this direction is to spread the approach to explicit objectives across all subjects, once one or two subjects have shown the way:

> *There is a need to implement all strategies further within a broader curriculum. I currently use the 'big picture' in geography and history, but aim to introduce it gradually into other curriculum areas.*

This can give a foundation for developing awareness about how learning generally can be improved. A primary school teacher was clear about this aspiration:

> *We aim to teach the core skills of taking responsibility for choices, making decisions, negotiating, resolving conflict, developing independence and self-esteem. We keep referring to these with the children, for example, praising them when they move in that direction or show those qualities.*

And a secondary school teacher gave an example of how this can be done, highlighting the ability to be well organized in carrying out a sequence of tasks:

> *Then we identified they needed to be much better organized, in their diaries.... It's mainly to look at their self-confidence and their literacy.... This spring term we have been preparing presentations on a topic they feel strongly about, e.g. animal testing, hunting, plastic surgery, etc. In pairs they have prepared a presentation and presented back to the group. After the half-term break we will start a new challenge. The idea is to carry out a strategy and then assess it, before moving on.*

So pupils can be helped to think about how they can direct and improve their own learning. Questions can probe 'What are we learning about what helps us learn? What hinders learning, and what can we do about that?' The more learners can be on the inside of these insights and decisions, the better.

Reflection 6.3

Check the scope of your pupils' learning intentions.

How subject-content-based are they?

My pupils' objectives and targets focus on areas which enrich and enhance their learning beyond subject content, for example:

. . . .

. . . .

. . . .

Consider whether there is a place for including more personal and social objectives or cross-curricular skills.

NEXT STEP

My pupils' objectives and targets can be broadened and deepened by:

. . . .

. . . .

. . . .

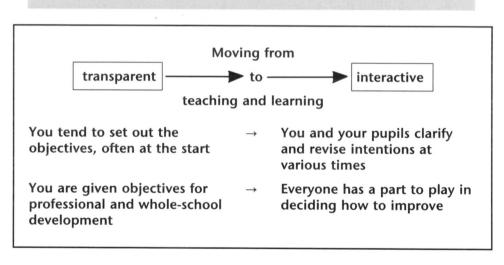

Moving from

| transparent | ⟶ to ⟶ | interactive |

teaching and learning

You tend to set out the objectives, often at the start → You and your pupils clarify and revise intentions at various times

You are given objectives for professional and whole-school development → Everyone has a part to play in deciding how to improve

Taking charge of professional and whole-school development

The principles that underpin pupils' learning in lessons apply equally to professional and whole-school development. Improvement appears to involve cycles of dissatisfaction, enquiry, planning, experimenting, sharing, doubting and persevering. Despite what some administrators suggest, the process is unpredictable and does not fit neat diagrams of plan-do-review. Success seems to depend on feeling in control and being clear about the rationale for change. Aims need to be periodically revisited and redefined in the light of experience. Success depends on colleagues having a voice in giving purpose and focus to their efforts to enhance provision.

An infant school deputy headteacher gave this review, typically emphasizing the value of a coherent, measured approach:

> There remains work to be done in including formative assessment strategies in planning. QCA documents show examples that are fairly low level, and present low expectations. The approach at (our school) would be to start with the individual child.... It's important not to try too much, the work has to progress one step at a time. There is still work to be done on learning intentions and success criteria, embedding the strategy into what children expect.

This was echoed by many colleagues, among them a junior school deputy headteacher:

> It is important that the school improvement plan continues to include these developments of AfL. It takes time to evolve the techniques.

Reflection 6.4

Check how staff members and teams work with leaders to set goals for development.

Is everyone clear about what the school sees as successful AfL, and how progress can be made?

We have these ways of setting our own agenda for professional and whole-school development:

. . . .

. . . .

. . . .

NEXT STEP

We can be more involved in giving direction to our development by:

. . . .

. . . .

. . . .

7 'What might be interesting about this?'

Working on INTEREST: connecting

- Building in fun, curiosity, challenge, relevance and control
- Identifying priorities for development and involving pupils

This chapter covers how interest provides a foundation both for pupils' learning and for professionals' development work. (Chapter 2 set the scene for this).

Building in fun, curiosity, challenge, relevance and control

Instinctively teachers know that learners' interest is a key to success. Interactive teachers try to bring to the surface what the appeal of a given topic or activity might be. At useful moments they can focus on learners' moods, tastes, preoccupations and aspirations. Transparent and interactive teaching tries to give pupils better reasons for doing things than 'We've got to do it' or 'It's on the national curriculum' or syllabus.

These secondary school pupils illustrate this:

If you do something fun, then you understand what you're doing more, instead of just copying things out of books.

If I don't really like it, I don't try my best. 'Cos it's a bit hard if you don't really like it. The better lessons are the fun ones. You do it better if you think it's fun.

My brother says it's the best invention he's ever seen, and it helps the environment because you don't drop paper cups everywhere. Designing and building it was fun. I messed up my Mum's kitchen a little bit while making it, but it was fun because my Dad helped me. And after I got it back I got a really good mark for it, and it made me feel I had done something really good for my homework, because I normally don't really put much effort into my homework.

Talking about what learners find interesting helps them develop their curiosity and motivation. One pupil's interest can ignite others'. It also helps teachers understand how activities might be given contexts which enhance pupils' enjoyment and commitment.

Coherence lends interest to a sequence of activities. Learners engage more readily when what they do hangs together and develops, rather than being bitty and disconnected. In the long run it does not help to give in to superficial preference for short, shallow, mechanistic tasks. Interactive teachers foster learners' interest by enabling them to contribute to the building of momentum and choice of direction.

These are a secondary school teacher's reflections on his way of trying to do some of these things:

> I'm under pressure to be efficient, but I'm not under pressure to be interesting. Are they fascinated? I've never been asked that question ever. . .
>
> Basically the philosophy is 'What do I have to do to make them remember this?' And usually the answer is to link it with their own experience, and obviously that can sometimes be impossible and/or tiresome and/or repetitive. . .
>
> Our mission statement, or similar, says INTEREST, RELEVANCE, SUCCESS. They're my planning principles, in that order.
>
> My Year 10 aren't going to get As or Bs, but they're all quite genned up on the difference between 'comprehension' and 'inference', on how to see two sides of a story. And I can actually talk to them about the construction of a piece of work. The bike analogy: I know they can ride a bike, not because I've lectured them on the parts and so on, but I can actually see them doing it. . . They're more capable of doing the work on their own, and they're more interested. . . . It has already begun to produce better results, better residuals and so on, better exam results. I'm convinced of it. They won't know quite as much about the Schlieffen plan as they did, they won't be able to go into the logistical detail, but they'll be able to construct two-sided essays, will be able to see points of similarity. . . and you can keep up the level of interest. . . .
>
> It's not going to stick in any meaningful way unless it's internalized. . . I'll give you a specific example. . . We were doing 'Why did people volunteer in World War I in the first two years; why did they stop volunteering?' . . . So I thought right, how do we do this? Well, the first thing we do is turn the books over and we guess reasons. Because I want them to see if they can pick it from their experience: you know, 'Why would you join up?' . . . We took the double page in the book, and I said 'Right, you find the other reasons on this page that we didn't have'. And then we had a five-minute discussion on 'Which ones would you fall for?' That's internalizing it. We're having a discussion about 'Would you fall for peer group pressure? If we got the white feather, what would we do?' So instead of making notes on the double page of the book, we highlighted the reasons and talked about them.

Another source of interest is the capacity learners have to make key decisions about what they do in lessons. Each of the options, explored throughout this chapter, offers a means by which learners can develop their own awareness and control of the tasks and projects they take on.

Learners can be sustained in their commitment to activity by developing a genuine, explicit understanding of what they are doing, hence what they are learning. What they are learning is revealed, and then supported, through consideration of prior knowledge, interest, intention, self-sufficiency, and so on. The more aware they are of these things, and of how to exploit them, the stronger will be their engagement, resourcefulness and achievement.

The more teachers and assistants can do to give learners responsibility for wondering, probing, asking questions, the better.

Reflection 7.1

Consider ways in which your pupils express, follow and develop their own interests.

My pupils have these ways of bringing their interests into lessons:

. . . .

. . . .

. . . .

Share ideas with colleagues about how pupils can be involved in planning lessons and topics.

NEXT STEP

We can improve pupils' interest in their learning by:

. . . .

. . . .

. . . .

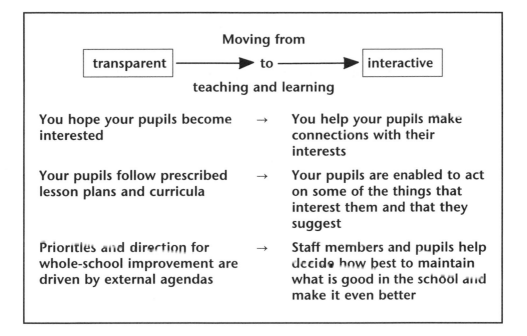

Moving from
transparent ——→ to ——→ interactive
teaching and learning

You hope your pupils become interested	→	You help your pupils make connections with their interests
Your pupils follow prescribed lesson plans and curricula	→	Your pupils are enabled to act on some of the things that interest them and that they suggest
Priorities and direction for whole-school improvement are driven by external agendas	→	Staff members and pupils help decide how best to maintain what is good in the school and make it even better

Identifying priorities for development and involving pupils

Schools which promote interactivity in whole-school development as well as in lessons are explicit about making connections between individual staff members' professional development and institutional changes. They also articulate connections between their own and other authorities' priorities for development.

> Infant school teacher: *We looked at how it would tie in with where we are as a school.*

> Infant school headteacher: *We started our children having a voice before it came onto the government's agenda. We know we are not there yet, but we are trying to make things coherent. There is a danger of operating things tangentially. We want pupil voice and assessment for learning all to become part of the school ethos.*

Reflection 7.2

Explore what you believe are priorities for individuals', teams' and whole-school development.

We are interested in these priorities for development:

. . . .

. . . .

. . . .

Explore what improvements your pupils might like to see in the curriculum. Do you have pupil representatives on working parties responsible for developing teaching and learning?

NEXT STEP

We can increase pupils' involvement in curriculum development by:

. . . .

. . . .

. . . .

8 'How can we know how well we do?'

> **Working on CRITERIA: understanding what counts as good**
> - Ways of developing and using criteria in lessons
> - Pupils use criteria
> - Using criteria in professional and whole-school development

This chapter covers the use of explicit criteria, in pupils' learning and in professionals' development, as a means of clarifying what to aim for, what progress is being made, and what to do next.

Ways of developing and using criteria in lessons

Developing understanding of criteria is a subtle and evolving part of learning, not a simple one-off event. Defining quality is one of the main challenges of AfL. There is no single way of using criteria that guarantees success. Teachers can be conscious, as this infant school teacher was, of avoiding rigid or mechanistic systems:

> *The idea is that explicit success criteria help the children, keep them focused, keep them on task, but I don't want it to be restrictive, for example, for the more able children.*

For some topics and subjects, criteria seem to fall into place quite quickly, whereas for others they are elusive. These infant school teachers were honest:

> *It's a struggle sometimes to unpick the task.*

> *It comes with practice: sometimes glaringly obvious, at other times you have to think hard.*

It helps to start with analysis of what pupils are currently capable of (see Chapter 5). Sometimes there is a long journey of personalized formative criteria before summative destinations can be approached.

One way of making criteria clear is for the teacher, teaching assistant or a pupil to model the performance. Another is for everyone to have examples of work to refer to, as this junior school teacher illustrated:

> *I do often tell the children how they can reach a level... or move onto the level above... but just prefer to ask the children to improve their work in comparison with the examples we are studying.*

These can be pieces of work by pupils on previous occasions or in other classes. They can be film clips, photos or recordings. They have strengths as well as weaknesses to learn from. Live models and sample pieces of work serve as criteria in action.

The important thing is for criteria to stimulate thinking, helping learners look forward to and look back on what they do. The pay-off is increased confidence, as these infant school teachers said:

> *Success criteria have helped to create a positive ethos within the classroom. It is good for self-esteem and positive behaviour.*

> *The success criteria are often cross-curricular, e.g. story writing in history. I explain in terms of 'I am looking for...' and 'I will be marking...' We are trying to shift attention from spelling and handwriting merely. I have had to teach myself not to be so presentation-oriented. I have just started using explicit success criteria in my **ICT** [Information communication technology] and **DT** [design technology] planning. We now make sure the children make their own success criteria, which they have done well. This has led to the development of a 'I have learnt' sheet, which they use to evaluate their achievement against the questions or points on the board.*

It is not always best to declare criteria at the outset. It can become too predictable and dull if routines are rigid, as this junior school teacher described:

> *I generate success criteria in different ways. Sometimes I tell the children, at other times I ask them to generate them at the start of the lesson, and sometimes I stop the children after twenty minutes working on a task and ask them what they think the success criteria should be.*

Criteria might well span more than one lesson, and so relate to medium-term objectives, rather than be restricted to what is required in any single task. An infant school teacher stated:

> *It may take time for some criteria to be worked on: a week or longer, for example. In other words it may not be necessary for criteria to be made afresh for each lesson.*

Criteria can refer to personal and social aspects of learning and to learning processes, as well as to subject content and learning outcomes. They can refer to the learners' preparation, motivation, confidence, stamina, method, in addition to any aspect of their conceptual understanding and skill performance.

This helps in decision-making about how many criteria there should be in any one instance, and about how to deal with on-going criteria. Some criteria can be generic and used for many activities in a subject. Examples of this are willingness to participate; handwriting and punctuation; presentation of self and work; linguistic or procedural accuracy; care with equipment and facilities; cooperation; and attention to the big picture, detail, criteria. Other criteria can be specific to the task and topic in hand. Some teachers make this a regular distinction, and have two sets of criteria for some activities.

A junior school teacher showed how constructive it is to see continuity and progression by referring back to criteria that have been used before:

> *Success criteria are now written with children, especially where they have covered an area before, and they are able to remember what they have to do to produce a good piece of work. This is a case of re-visiting and reinforcing, practising and refining.*

And a junior school pupil understood the process:

> *Sometimes we do the draft, and then Miss asks us all what we have included, and then we make the list of success criteria to be used for the best piece.*

Different pupils in a class may use different criteria, as this infant school teacher said:

> *Groups of pupils may have different criteria to work on, while the overall intention is common to all.*

Being explicit about criteria can stop marking from being sterile or obscure (see Appendix 4 for more information about marking policy, and Appendix 8 for an example of marking dialogue). This primary school teaching assistant was one among many who saw the advantages of using explicit criteria:

> *It makes the focus clearer when I'm marking.*

Using criteria rigorously and sensitively can transform feedback from a check on defects and deficits into the recognition of success and guidance toward further improvement. Constructive use of criteria turns a judge into a coach.

Being clear about criteria is the foundation for pupils' self and peer assessment. It means learners can build on achievement and know how to improve (see Chapters 11 and 12).

Learners, assistants and teachers can select criteria for themselves. They may choose criteria that apply in national tests and qualifications. But they can equally concentrate on whatever they find helpful to the learning at any given time.

Criteria do not have to be set by public authorities. Criteria can be:

- public or national (e.g. level or grade descriptions, or a formal markscheme);
- the teacher's (e.g. *I want you to concentrate today on...*);
- the pupil's (e.g. *Most important to me in this activity is...*);
- a pupil group's (e.g. *We decided...*);
- the whole class's (e.g. *Our objective is to...*);
- a specific audience's/client's (e.g. *Class 3 wants a story which...*);
- borrowed from, or simulating, a real-life or hypothetical context (e.g. *To improve the layout of our car-park...; We'll work as if in a television studio*).

Criteria come to life when learners use them to solve problems, to assess themselves and one another, and to decide how to improve. Using criteria formatively means learners can:

- diagnose strengths and weaknesses in their own and others' performance;
- decide what to do next, what to change, or when to stop their activity;
- decide what teaching and support they would like to help them with what they are doing and learning;
- devise their own criteria for an activity;
- transfer criteria taken from one context of activity to another;
- question the source and suitability of criteria;
- evaluate and amend criteria.

This secondary school teacher spoke for several newly trained colleagues who felt at home with these strategies:

> *Perhaps because I'm recently trained, a lot of it seems quite intuitive to me:*
> - *making criteria clear and explicit*
> - *making models available and observing performances*
> - *identifying good qualities*
> - *identifying areas for improvement.*
> *We're trying to get them to find their own way. If they know the strengths and*

weaknesses in their own work, they know there are things they can do about it. I can give them scaffolding to help them get there, but it doesn't mean I'm being didactic. It's more self-awareness... If it comes from them, it's not as judgemental.

And a junior school colleague explained:

This is a way of working I have now developed:
- *state a learning objective;*
- *analyse the relevant performance, say, a text to identify the essential features that make it good (e.g. why is this report a good report; why is this two-sided argument a fair presentation of a contentious issue?);*
- *suggest some success criteria for the task in hand and finalize those with the pupils, or ask the pupils to create their own and explain them;*
- *pupils colour code each of the success criteria;*
- *carry out the activity;*
- *peer pupil, pupil her/himself and/or teacher marks the work, using the colour coding, e.g. underlining sections in orange that fulfil the orange success criterion;*
- *peer pupil, pupil her/himself, and/or teacher prompts improvement in terms of one or more of the success criteria;*
- *pupils have time and support, if appropriate, to improve their performance.*

Reflection 8.1

Reflect on how you enable your pupils to use criteria.

When do they work well?

Share experiences with colleagues about how criteria are used:

- to prepare and launch activities;
- during activities;
- in marking;
- in pupils' self and peer assessment;
- to help improve performance;
- to help prepare for summative assessments.

We have these ways of enabling pupils to use criteria to inform and enhance their learning:

. . . .

. . . .

. . . .

Collect some of your pupils' perceptions about using criteria. Do they suggest any improvements?

Consider how your pupils' use of criteria might help them become more independent.

NEXT STEP

We can improve our pupils' use of criteria by:

. . . .

. . . .

. . . .

Pupils use criteria

The clearer teachers, assistants *and* pupils are about criteria for what they are doing, the better. Teachers, assistants and pupils can learn together about how to define quality in their work. An infant school teacher saw this as a breakthrough:

> *The bureaucratic recording of success criteria on planning sheets could be eliminated, because a better approach was for the pupils to work with their teacher to specify their own success criteria.*

Explicit criteria help pupils develop a sense of purpose, satisfaction and autonomy. These primary school pupils summed up:

> *Success criteria help us to get on with our work without putting our hand up all the time.*

I like giving the success criteria, because I can say what I think I should be learning.

I look back and check that I've done them all.

When you've finished, you ask a friend to look through and check you've not missed anything out.

I can see when I have done it properly.

Success criteria tell us what we should have achieved by the end of the lesson.

Perhaps because of their teaching, some secondary school pupils related the use of criteria more specifically to test and exam performance:

You can see what the teachers are looking for, so you can see what you've got to do.

It's helpful, but it puts pressure on you.

When you get the sheet, it says to get this grade, like 5b or c, right up to 7, and I really want to get a 7. That's what you mainly look at, that's what I want to achieve. But you don't achieve it and you feel bad with yourself and you beat yourself up about it.

Chapter 10 is about dealing with difficulty, and offers ways of handling and forestalling feelings of failure.

The essential question is 'What do you think makes clear whether this is well done or not?' Pupils helping to define criteria becomes the key development for interactive teachers. The direction is clear, even if progress takes time, as this infant school teacher explained:

I have begun to ask the pupils, e.g. about independent writing, 'What do you need to do to be successful or really good?' They said capital letters, full stops, neat handwriting, and so on. The plan was for them to sign up to specific success criteria, but there was not enough time, so I decided for them and pinned them on the wall. I thought there would be no interest, but they were very interested when they saw their names. I will continue with this next half term.

More successfully, a primary school teacher demonstrated this in a lesson, speaking to her class:

We're going to try and make this story easier so someone who is 4 or 5 could understand it. I've written some of the things you have to think about on the board for when you are trying to do it:
  - *Consider your audience (think about our last lesson)*

- *Use the thesaurus to make words easier*
- *Simplify sentences.*

Can you come up with some rules to simplify sentences? Talk to the person next to you, and I'll ask for ideas in a minute.

Two more primary school colleagues described how these processes were developing:

> *We had a lesson specifically on problem solving in maths, discussing 'What do you need to know?' The pupils came up with a list, and then we discussed 'How do you do each of those things?' This gave a focus to the teaching and in my marking I could refer to the list, using the pupils' words. All of this fits together: the success criteria, the teaching, the marking, the talking with pupils at their table groups, and so on.*

> *There is a feeling that early work has been consolidated. Initially children were given the success criteria, and staff shared success criteria which were written on the planning sheet. Now, they are left off the planning sheet as staff gained confidence in the use of success criteria, and increasingly the children are coming up with them in the course of the lesson.*

A secondary school teacher explained how she came to this approach:

> *Recently I was writing essay questions for my Year 11s: 'Why am I writing essay questions? Why can't they write essay questions?' And I realized well actually they can. They know the criteria, they know what the themes are, they can write their own essay questions. Shortly I'll be redundant, because there's not a lot I can do once I've shared with them skills, not a lot they can't do if led in the right direction.*

And another secondary school teacher described what has become a typical procedure:

> *What we're doing now is I'm getting them to write their own criteria, so, for example, we've done the poetry, I've said 'This is the theme, you could well be asked a question on this theme, what question will they ask you?' And they start with 'Oh I don't know' and then you say 'Well, what skills do they have to test you on?' which they already know because they've looked at the criteria. And they actually come up with the question and the bullet points, because it's fairly straightforward really, and they start thinking like examiners. It's almost like a mind shift.*

It is noticeable how the important questions are given to the learners to answer. This is interactive teaching, designed to promote analysis and autonomy. It is a different kind of 'teaching the test' from what is normally meant by that expression. The pupils are learning how to understand and meet requirements. They are gaining insight and control in such a way that they can apply those lessons to other activities, such as when the outcome is not a summative assessment but their own pleasure, their own creativity, or a service provided for others.

Reflection 8.2

Consider what part your pupils play in deciding their own criteria.

My pupils set criteria in these ways:

. . . .

. . . .

. . . .

Share examples with colleagues of how pupils might have more of a voice in selecting and setting criteria.

NEXT STEP

We can increase our pupils' decision-making about criteria by:

. . . .

. . . .

. . . .

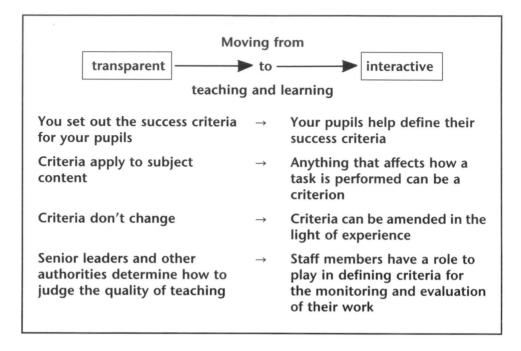

Moving from

transparent ——————▶ to ——————▶ interactive

teaching and learning

You set out the success criteria for your pupils →	Your pupils help define their success criteria
Criteria apply to subject content →	Anything that affects how a task is performed can be a criterion
Criteria don't change →	Criteria can be amended in the light of experience
Senior leaders and other authorities determine how to judge the quality of teaching →	Staff members have a role to play in defining criteria for the monitoring and evaluation of their work

Using criteria in professional and whole-school development

Understanding criteria belongs to good subject knowledge and good leadership.

When a teacher relies on someone else's planning, there can be a problem. Inheriting someone else's definition of criteria for a task can mean the teacher has not really thought through what is involved. It can be uncomfortable when learners raise issues that deviate from what was planned. As this infant school teacher commented:

> *The trickiest part is the success criteria, especially when one colleague does the planning for another.*

By the same token, leaders and staff members have to engage with and own the criteria by which their work is guided and evaluated. This means getting on the inside of public criteria. A very effective way of doing this is to create your own criteria and to map those onto ones you are obliged to recognize.

Many teachers have found that they have to change how they define criteria, so as to prevent their pupils from finding routines dull. There seems to be no single guaranteed method of communicating criteria. The same applies to professional and whole-school development (see Appendix 9).

Sometimes literacy and numeracy dominate, but criteria apply in all subjects. In some schools criteria are being used to guide and record learning in personal, social and extra-curricular areas of learning. We found that our confident schools developed case studies of different subject areas. These help establish common principles, while respecting diversity of teaching styles and subject cultures.

Common approaches have to be discussed with teaching assistants and trainee colleagues. A junior school deputy headteacher noted:

> *The SCITT student who has been working with the class has been able to take on the use of success criteria in her teaching. Pupils were very positive about this in interviews.*

Primary school staff members used part of a whole-school INSET day to agree these criteria for evaluating spoken and written feedback across the school. They stated that they see the confidence, resilience and independence they aim to develop, when their *pupils:*

- *listen attentively to the teacher's and one another's feedback;*
- *are willing to engage in dialogue about their learning;*
- *can say what they are doing well and what this looks like in their work;*
- *can say what they need to improve and how they will do this;*
- *show that they have taken the feedback comments and worked to incorporate ideas or improve their work in the next task;*
- *can show another pupil and/or the teacher that their work has improved as a result of feedback and acting on it.*

These illustrate how criteria can be used to plan, implement and evaluate classroom and whole-school developments. (See Chapter 14 pages 134–5 for more whole-school evaluative questions.)

Reflection 8.3

Consider how you currently use criteria to promote your own development: as an individual, in your team(s), and as a whole school.

We have these ways of using criteria to inform development:

. . . .

. . . .

. . . .

NEXT STEP

We can improve the use of criteria in planning and evaluating our professional and whole-school development by:

. . . .

. . . .

. . . .

9 'How do we tackle it?'

Working on METHOD: knowing what to do

- Having different ways of learning what to do
- Making your method of development your own

As the previous chapter shows, being clear about criteria helps learners know what they are aiming for and how to judge progress. This chapter looks at ways of being clear about how to carry out activities. And what applies to pupils in lessons is true also for adults in professional and whole-school development.

Having different ways of learning what to do

This is about questions such as 'What do I have to do? How do I do it?' Teachers whose aim is to promote learners' autonomy pass these questions back. They prompt learners to find their own answers as far as possible: by talking to one another; by checking instructions or guidance; by reviewing objectives. The principle here is getting the learners to do the work, rather than making things easy for them. Reduced challenge means diminished satisfaction (see Appendix 8).

Transparent and interactive teaching gives pupils props such as these to support their activities and learning:

- examples to work from;
- checklists of steps to take;
- defined roles, particularly for paired or group activities;
- timetables to work to;
- ways of analysing other people's performances (see Chapter 8);
- ways of recognizing what they do well (see Chapter 11);
- time, support and guidance to make improvements (see Chapter 12).

Specifying instructions too fully or too rigidly runs the risk of making activities overly comfortable and predictable. So when there is a checklist for an activity, or roles are assigned, or a timetable is used, discussion can take issue with how effective the specification turns out to be.

Effective teachers and learners are prepared to make and revise multiple pragmatic decisions about how they perform. In order to know what to do, teachers and learners have to be more dynamic and responsive to the moment than they can be in respect of the criteria they use for defining aim and quality of outcome. Criteria require more articulate, analytic judgement.

When things go wrong, there are several sorts of explanation. It may have to do with effort (see Chapters 7 and 10). The intention may be flawed (see Chapters 6 and 8), or the implementation. It is also possible that resources are lacking, having an effect on method. When method is the focus, learners consider: are they taking suitable steps; are they taking the steps properly? If things turn out well, learners can consolidate their learning by asking 'What helped that work? How can I have that success in future?'

The most effective way of giving learners these kinds of insight is to enable them to own the methods they use in their activities. Transparency in teaching is the first step. Interactivity translates adherence to prescribed method into practical understanding and initiative.

This first school teacher described how he works:

> *I tell them what their success criteria are, and ask them to decide for themselves how to set about the task. This gives them some independence, but makes clear what they are aiming for.*

Learners may well have to mimic and borrow at the start and from time to time, but the aim is for them to use their knowledge, understanding and skill in academic and real-life contexts when they need and want to.

It is a feature of complex and craft skills that certain things have to be taken for granted. Learners can pay attention to no more than a small number of the competences that combine to make up the tasks they tackle in school. It is a mark of proficient practitioners to be no more than tacitly aware of many facets of what they do. The novice brings these facets of performance into focal awareness in order to acquire, rehearse and refine them. It is the role of coaching to assist this.

Formative assessment provides feedback on which bits of the method are working, and which need more attention, or less. But pupils sometimes rely too much on teachers and others, sparing themselves effort. This sixth form teacher explained:

> *With some groups I find it difficult to open up the question of 'method': how are we going to do this? Because the students seem to be confused by choice and variety. They seem to think it's down to the teacher to decide how to do things. They seem to think the method is mine, and they just want me to tell them how we're doing it so they can get on with it. It is a real challenge to help them take ownership.*

A junior school teacher was careful to distinguish between 'method' and 'criteria':

> *If you're modelling something, you're modelling how to do something, and then you can pull out what it is you've done that has enabled you to do that, and that's how you get your success criteria. Unpicking the success criteria from the learning objective is how we look at it. 'Method' suggests more of a task approach to me – 'How shall we go and do it then?' For example, 'Get your books out. . .', or in a science investigation 'Set up apparatus', and so on. Success criteria state what will achieve the purpose, whereas the method is more activity-based. If you think of something like maths, problem solving, there will be certain things I want, and I ask the children to approach it in a way that suits them. So long as I can see the method is appropriate, they have made a bigger decision than if I say I want it done by 'Two by two digit'. . . It's lovely to see what they do: they approach things in ways that probably I wouldn't think of, and you can see where their thinking is. And a lot of it is to do with confidence: if they have confidence in that method, they can continue to use it. Whereas if there's a method they're not happy with, they may not go that way that time. There may be a lesson in the course of a week when I'm teaching a specific method, and then I would want to see that and to see what they can do with it. And then if there's a problem-solving activity by the end of the week, they would have a choice.*

This secondary school teacher described how he changed his method of teaching and learning, while retaining focus on explicit GCSE criteria:

> *I attended an AfL secondary link teachers' meeting, when the colleague from _____ School reported on their work in history. I came back. . . and ripped up what I was going to do, took my class down to the library, told them 'We've got to study a pre-1914 novel and we've got to look at character and so on; you go and find what you're interested in' and we ended up with a room full of books. That reminded me what English was supposed to be about. Not photocopies of 'What I want you to read', but books. And then we had three weeks of people reading, which was weird!. . . We negotiated the questions to work on. . . They were finding out for themselves.*

How good method is becomes clear in practice. How good criteria are becomes clear in judgement. The two come together when identifying strengths (see Chapter 11), and when making improvements (see Chapter 12).

When learners have followed a good enough method well enough, they complete their activity. The achievement has to be satisfactory at least. But if they want to achieve the best results, they need to do more than follow secure procedures. They need to engage with and understand criteria for quality, and be prepared to adapt method to circumstance and moment accordingly. Method takes learning only so far. Criteria fulfil learning.

Reflection 9.1

Consider the different ways your pupils have of finding out and checking how to do the tasks they have. What visual prompts do they have? Who can they talk to?

My pupils have these ways of knowing what to do:

. . . .

. . . .

. . . .

NEXT STEP

My pupils can take greater control over how they carry out their activities by:

. . . .

. . . .

. . . .

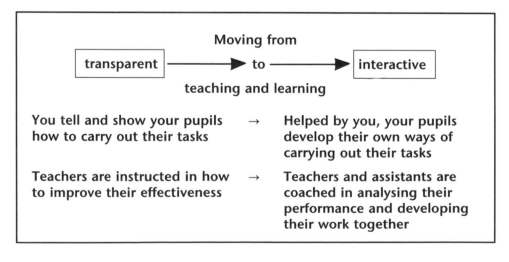

Moving from

transparent ⟶ to ⟶ interactive

teaching and learning

You tell and show your pupils how to carry out their tasks	→	Helped by you, your pupils develop their own ways of carrying out their tasks
Teachers are instructed in how to improve their effectiveness	→	Teachers and assistants are coached in analysing their performance and developing their work together

Making your method of development your own

Just as pupils can make their method for performing tasks their own, so can staff members make their method of developing their practice their own.

Here a junior school teacher described how classroom experimentation became a method of whole-school development:

> *AfL has proved useful, so colleagues are using it, whereas they bin other initiatives. The more I work with this, the more it becomes owned by the children. For example, if I'm having a bad day and I get to the end of a lesson, they say to me 'Excuse me; let's just self assess this', or 'We are going to mark it, aren't we?' They want to know how well they've done. My practice is evolving through a greater sense of self assessment and peer assessment. The more I do it, the more they get involved. I train them early on in self assessment. I wasn't rigid, deliberately, because different children self assess in different ways. For example, some colour code the **WILF** ['what I'm looking for'] and highlight the text according to the colour; other children use a numerical code; some use brackets. So it's not 'You'll do it like this'. I've given the ownership to them, and so they enjoy it. They can see the purpose of it. After that I give them feedback, and it's incredibly easy to do: either I agree or I disagree. If there's a need to improve the work, I highlight that. We don't always agree. My phrase is 'Next time you need to. . .' or 'Next time try to. . .'; it's not a 'But. . .' because it's like when we get feedback on lessons, you get all the plus points and you're waiting for the 'But'. Sometimes I'll write 'The unsuccessful part' and draw a line down and say something like 'Continue this sentence with. . .' After their self assessment and my feedback, I like to see a response from the child, every time where appropriate. What's happening is that – not always, but quite a lot – coverage is getting in the way: you move on. Even if it's the same topic, there's that sense of 'What's on the plan? Better get onto that.' It goes back to culture and habit. We teachers are so in the mould of blocks. The thing is when is 'Next time'? When will it be?*
>
> *I've not gone as far yet as _____ (colleague). With mine, it's gone from me giving them success criteria for certain activities, and the children have to come up with the WILF, from which they can then see where they're going and why.*
>
> *On four boys' books I wrote WILF because they hadn't been writing in full sentences. They looked at it, and one of them said 'I can see exactly what I haven't done.' Hey hey, we're getting somewhere with this! And I said 'We are going to be doing another comprehension later in the week', and he said 'Yes, and I'll know how to do it then to do it properly'. But this opportunity was a one-off, because the other children were reading quietly. It's about how we make that a habit.*
>
> *Our timetable will change in September and we'll have extended lessons when*

you can do review sessions, and the kids will pick up on that, and know 'Now we're doing review and improve'.

*And this way of working will turn our planning on its head. Our planning is normally 'input, devise criteria, go and do, and then review in the plenary'. But you'd have to look at putting that review process at the top, unless you deal with it as something separate. And you can do 'review and improve' for literacy, but can you do it for maths, history, geography...? I think you'd have to adapt it for every lesson, if you were going to do it well. We are not rewarded for changing our plans. But I keep hearing that people in **Ofsted** like messy plans.*

This teacher was used to sharing and comparing how he and his colleagues work. He sees patterns and possibilities in development, which are taken on in changes to whole-school organization.

Reflection 9.2

Consider how you use formative assessment to make teaching and learning effective. How do you share ideas and experiences about this? How are your methods of formative assessment communicated to new colleagues?

NEXT STEP

We can improve how we inform ourselves and other people about our methods of formative assessment by:

. . . .

. . . .

. . . .

10 'What can we do when we get stuck or go wrong?'

Working on RESILIENCE: what to do about not knowing

- Having ways of dealing with uncertainty
- Learning to welcome difficulty
- Feeling secure in action research

This chapter covers how learners can be helped to cope with, and even benefit from, difficulty. The last section applies the same principles to professional and whole-school development.

Having ways of dealing with uncertainty

Perhaps the first resource pupils can have, when they face a problem, is one or more of their peers. Interactive teachers use a range of means to enable learners to support and challenge one another.

One set of strategies for this can be summed up as 'learning partners'. These include talk partners and response partners (see Chapter 4). The benefit is that in one-to-one dialogue a learner has access to mirroring, sounding board and feedback.

These primary school pupils spoke from their experience:

If you are at amber, you might just talk to the person next to you.

When trying something that is difficult, friends can help.

And this infant school pupil understood why:

If you get stuck, you can talk to the person sat next to you or some of the other people in the group. That way you don't have to ask the teacher all the time.

Interactive teachers find practical ways of communicating with their pupils about plans, progress and what to do about queries and snags. Posters, for example, explain steps to be taken when in difficulty. Learning or working walls display mind-maps, intentions, questions and directions for research, work in progress and finished products. These serve to strengthen learners' desire to overcome problems. (See Appendix 8 for a case study, and Chapter 6 for more ways of referring to objectives for guidance.)

This infant school pupil described his classroom:

> *There are resources around the room that can help if you get stuck, or if something is difficult. In literacy there is the alphabet on the wall, and in numeracy there is the number line that can help.*

A primary school pupil was used to referring to prompts and support around the classroom:

> *When we were doing puzzles today, I looked on the wall and got some help from the poster with pictures, and sorted it out for myself.*

And a junior school pupil similarly had helpful routines:

> *When we get stuck we refer back to the 'remember to's. They help us understand and achieve our work. Being visible, they help because you don't have to remember, you just look at the board.*

Another junior school pupil came to this confident conclusion:

> *The whiteboards are good because you can work things out, and if you find it difficult, you can rule out what you've done and start again. You can have as many goes as you like.*

Interactive and effective teachers help their pupils build these strategies into their learning. An infant school teacher gave this example:

> *We have displays on the classroom walls with prompts: 'What do you need more help with? What are you finding difficult? What are you finding easy? Do you have any questions?' I use these to ask children to review their work. Once they have thought about these questions, I respond with ideas for them to try.*

And a primary school teacher described this approach:

> *At the start of the year the group mapped ideas about 'Why do we come to school?' The ideas that the class gave were then used to create a list of 'Our jobs' and the 'Teacher's jobs'. These refer to what should be done where work is difficult.*

All of this is about one of the most important questions that teachers and learners can ask: 'What do we do when we don't know?'

Reflection 10.1

Check what ways your pupils have of dealing with hitches and glitches. How are they helped to use routines and resources to learn through difficulty?

My pupils have these ways of relying on themselves and one another:

. . . .

. . . .

. . . .

How could they be helped to be even more independent and interdependent? Collect a range of strategies to help pupils develop resilience and perseverance.

NEXT STEP

My pupils can become more self-sufficient by:

. . . .

. . . .

. . . .

Learning to welcome difficulty

Summative assessment undermines the proper risk-taking and tolerance of ambiguity that formative assessment tries to develop. It takes courage to stick with complexity and forego the temptation of the short-term and superficial.
A junior school pupil summed it up very well:

> *You have to be stuck sometimes because, if everything was easy, you wouldn't learn new things.*

Many teachers who engage with the theory and practice of formative assessment find that an essential part of what they are trying to do is to foster brave and resilient attitudes in their pupils. Getting stuck and making mistakes can be welcomed. Determination and willingness to try alternatives are highly prized.

These infant school pupils understood well enough:

It doesn't matter if it doesn't work the first time.

We have to think about how the lesson was sometimes. It's good because you get to say if you're stuck.

Sometimes we have to do independent work, and you try and figure it out for yourself.

Similarly in primary schools, there were pupils who have learned these important lessons for life:

Miss says that if you find it difficult, you're learning.

When we get stuck, we don't worry or panic, because thinking hard is new learning.

If you got it all right, there would be no point coming to school.

They have a school culture such as this, described by an infant school headteacher:

We have always been positive about encountering difficulty: to struggle is good. All of the children are encouraged to have a go and are not criticized for making mistakes.

In order to encourage such a culture, interactive teachers present themselves as human beings, capable of uncertainty and error, ready to listen to criticism and advice. As a junior school teacher said:

I have been trying to change this culture of being afraid to make mistakes, by sharing my personal experience of learning and encountering difficulties.

A secondary school teacher explained the change in pupils' attitudes:

Rather than saying 'I don't get it, tell me again', they're actually asking informed questions. They're asking 'This is what I've done, is this right?' or 'When you said such-and-such, does it mean that we have to. . .?' So that they're taking on board what they have to do, rather than doing the hands-up-in-horror 'I don't get any of it and frankly I'd rather not engage my brain cells at all'.

Confidence to live with and learn from uncertainty depends on constructive dialogue and good working relationships. At the heart of this are learners' attitudes toward themselves and their views of what it means to learn. Interactive teachers offer a perception of ability not as something innate and fixed, but as something everyone can develop (see Chapter 2).

Reflection 10.2

Consider what your pupils believe about 'getting it right'.

Share with colleagues, ways of assuring your pupils that mistakes and problems help them learn.

We have these ways of increasing our pupils' confidence to risk error and deal with uncertainty:

. . . .

. . . .

. . . .

NEXT STEP

Our pupils can be helped to be more resilient by:

. . . .

. . . .

. . . .

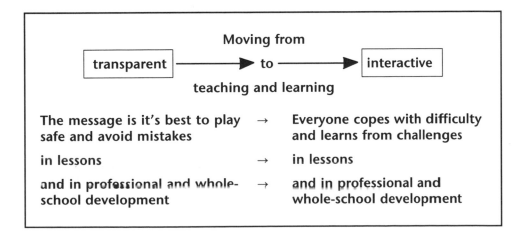

Feeling secure in action research

Being confident enough to admit things are not going as planned is part of a school's as well as a classroom's ethos. An infant school teacher appreciated the trust and freedom she felt she was allowed:

> *I am very pleased to be able to explore with my class how things are going, to involve them in thinking about what works. I like the flexibility that comes with this project. In my first year of teaching I was scared to divert from the plan. Now in my second year I am enjoying this development.*

Teachers are enabled to develop such confidence by having leaders, managers, advisers and inspectors, who encourage them to innovate and not be afraid of learning as they go. An infant school deputy headteacher summed up her experience:

> *It has been useful to talk without feeling that there is a right or wrong answer. There has been an acceptance that not everything is going to work perfectly. It is a learning process to be developed at our own pace.*

This approach to professional and school development differs from a traditional style of 'Do as you're told' or 'Just implement these proven strategies'. A junior school headteacher explained:

> *AfL training is different to other training we experience. Many questions are asked, but few answers given. It is a process of development. There will be problems along the way, but look on them as challenges to be overcome. Challenge accepted practice. Constantly self evaluate. Keep learning and challenge yourself.*

Reflection 10.3

Check what messages your team gives and receives about experiment and innovation. Are trial and error welcomed as part of the process?

We have these ways of encouraging confidence to change as professionals:

. . . .

. . . .

. . . .

Consider what can be done to strengthen the view that continuing professional and whole-school development is collaborative and adventurous.

NEXT STEP

We can be more resilient and resourceful in our development work by:

. . . .

. . . .

. . . .

11 'What have we achieved?'

Working on ACHIEVEMENT: appreciating what goes well

- Feedback, self and peer assessment
- Giving praise a focus
- Feeling the buzz
- Recording achievement
- First take account of strengths

This chapter is about recognizing and building on success. These are vital to pupils' learning, as well as to professionals' and schools' development.

Feedback, self and peer assessment

Photographic records, taping, displays and portfolios are ways of bringing attention to what learners accomplish. This is the most direct form of feedback: the evidence speaks for itself. And the more involvement learners have in highlighting the positive features in their progress and achievement, the stronger will be their motivation to carry on learning.

Assessment interprets the evidence. How it is done has a powerful effect on learners and how they feel about learning.

Formative assessment helps pupils learn to appreciate the progress they and their peers make. An infant school deputy headteacher described the cycles of effort and celebration she and her class have developed:

> *If you've shared with them at the beginning, in the plenary you can ask 'Have you done what we talked about?' Better than just packing up. And now the children expect it, and ask 'So can I bring it back and share?'*

Criteria can appear abstract, so model pieces of work can be used to illustrate them. When they compare their own efforts with examples of work carried out by others, and analyse these according to criteria, learners realize what they have achieved.

Transparency is the first step: being clear about the quality of what is being aimed for. An infant school teacher, for example, was sure that using criteria made her marking more efficient:

Focused marking has been developed where the learning focus is written at the top of the page, and comments refer back to this. This has cut down on the time spent marking, and has meant that there is more purpose to the marking.

And a junior school teacher spoke for many, agreeing that:

My marking is a lot more focused, a lot easier and a lot quicker. I wouldn't highlight every single day. I might highlight it, and then just put a face at the bottom.

Interactivity is the second step: giving the learners a role in assessment, and prompting them to do something with it. This is often accompanied by the use of colour and inventive ways of highlighting successes and areas for improvement. A junior school teacher showed how this can be done:

Children have been using the traffic light system to make judgements about their learning, both orally during lessons, on whiteboards and on written pieces of work. Asking children to add comment to the colour they have given is very revealing. For example, one child who is good at maths gave himself a green light and had all the work correct. While it may have seemed that he had progressed little through the lesson, his comment was 'I struggled when I got to the larger numbers'. He had to evaluate his learning in more detail through giving comment.

One of the most important implications is that pupils spend more time making assessments themselves, and must have more time to benefit from their feedback than was customary in the past. 'Comment marking' is wasted if it is not followed up. An infant school teacher explained:

Time needs to be made for pupils to use important pieces of marking, e.g. at routine settling-down times early on or after breaks, and/or at special times such as a Friday when catch-up, follow-up and extension work can be done. This might involve parents/carers sometimes.

Pupils get non-verbal and spoken feedback about their performance from their teachers and others. They can also assess themselves and one another, using explicit criteria as a guide. Most teachers discover they need to 'train' their pupils in self and peer assessment, as this junior school teacher said:

During plenaries children look at one another's work, and give feedback. It takes some time to get beyond the stage of 'It was good'. Children need to develop the language to evaluate their work. To solve this it is important that there is lots of modelling to show children the kinds of comment they could make.

As more and more pupils become familiar with these processes, more and more teachers will be able to capitalize on pupils' ability to assess their own and one another's achievements. In interactive lessons these questions are commonplace: 'What is going well? How can it be even better?' This has given rise to a classroom acronym: **EBI**, standing for 'Even better if...' which encourages learners to work out how to build on what they have done so far.

Many teachers who have engaged with AfL have found it helps always to be constructive and to bias comments in favour of the positive. Some use 'two stars and a wish', for example, or two or three successes for every point to work further on. This is not to avoid rigour. It is to build on existing capability (see Chapter 5). A junior school pupil described the process he and his classmates were using:

> We do a piece of writing, and when we think we might have finished, we get the correction pens and check what we have done. They help us remember what we need to think about if we are going to do our work well. This means you don't forget what you have to do.

An infant school teacher had a special way of asking her pupils for their assessment:

> I have a play phone and I call individual pupils and ask them about what they have been doing, what they have found hard, and what they feel they have done well. They then pass the phone on to another child of their choosing.

These infant school pupils knew how to signal how well they think they are doing:

> If we think something's easy we put our hand like that (thumb up), if we're not really sure we do that (thumb horizontal), and if we haven't got a clue at all we put our thumb down.

> When we think something's good or sort of good, for 'good' we put a green dot in the corner, if it's 'sort of good' you put an orange dot, and if you don't like it at all you put a red dot.

A secondary school teacher summed up:

> It's changed the way a lot of us think about assessment. What you used to think sounded like a cop-out: 'Oh I'll get the pupils to do it'. But it is actually a quite sophisticated negotiating process, involving lots of new knowledge on both the pupils' and your parts.

And here is an illustration from a lesson. This is a secondary school teacher, speaking to the class, giving guidance on the peer marking of a whole project as a lead-in to target setting:

> Look back in your sketchbooks. You've done various tonal portraits. You've done a self-portrait. Also you looked at profile portraits. You did some critical studies looking at Picasso. And you ended up completing an A3 distorted fragmented portrait, based on the work of Picasso. . . . I want you to mark them looking at the positives: 'What have I achieved?' I want you to write down three things you're pleased with, and then two areas that you're not so happy with. Once you've done that, we're going to come up with a target for improvement. For this, refer to the back of your sketchbook where there's the grid, remember. Look down the grid. If you award yourself a level 5, what can you do to get to a level 6? You need to look down the targets: see what you need to do to develop to the next level.

Reflecting on this after the lesson, she commented:

> The feedback they received from their friends is perhaps in more detail than they would get if I was marking the work. And they've got two or three people reviewing the work, rather than just one person's opinion of what they've done. They take a lot more notice of each other's comments when they know that their friends are going to be looking at their work, because they knew that right from the beginning. I think that helped them make sure their work really was an awful lot better that it would have been if they were submitting it just to me to mark.

Reflection 11.1

Check the different ways your pupils have of appreciating what they achieve.

My pupils have these ways of identifying what they do well:

. . . .

. . . .

. . . .

Consider the balance in the feedback your pupils get.

Is the emphasis on strengths and successes, or on shortcomings and failures?

My pupils receive feedback with these main features:

. . . .

. . . .

. . . .

NEXT STEP

My pupils can better highlight their progress and achievement by:

. . . .

. . . .

. . . .

Giving praise a focus

It is important to find out about how your pupils regard rewards, what they think of their own abilities, and whether they believe they can ever learn to direct and judge their own activities. It helps learners to see that success depends on effort and resourcefulness, rather than on innate ability or reliance on others. They learn more and better when they change 'Have I done it OK?' into 'What have I done well in this?' followed up by 'Can I make it even better?'

There is challenging research that suggests reward and motivation that are extrinsic undermine authentic confidence and autonomy (see Chapter 2 pages 13–4). But some teachers are not keen to dispense with merits, stars, badges and privileges such as the opportunity to choose activities. Here are four infant school teachers talking about this:

> *I can't go completely against extrinsic rewards: it's part of social learning which starts concrete and becomes more abstract. It depends on the developmental stage. Rewards can bridge a gap in emotional development.*
>
> *It's hard to think what intrinsic rewards alone would look like. We emphasize*

the completing of tasks. Intrinsic reward depends on there being a language of emotion and support surrounding the child, and requires a sophisticated understanding of the messages being conveyed.

Very young children seem to combine the two [intrinsic and extrinsic reward]. *There is an encouraging language of 'We're very pleased' today.*

Children can work for a sticker and work for you, then begin to succeed and say 'Yes, I can. . . .'

But this infant school teacher took a different view:

I try not to use stickers, as I feel that the children are inappropriately motivated by them. They serve to distract from the learning.

An infant school deputy headteacher saw the dilemma:

I have tried to reduce my use of external rewards. This has proven difficult as some children are on programmes where this is encouraged. For example, if they complete a task or session, they receive a reward. Increasingly it is becoming part of our culture that young people question 'What am I going to get?'

The question is: do praise and rewards positively reinforce achievement, or do they weaken the will to try alternatives and continue learning?

One of the most respected teachers in our project had this approach:

I don't praise my pupils when they've done something. I set them another challenge.

These junior school pupils knew what they thought:

We like to get praise. Stamps aren't enough.

And we need to know how to improve.

What seems crucial is that learners have criteria and opportunities to use them in a range of ways. Criteria determine 'What am I aiming for?' and 'How well did I do?' They shift the source of praise or reward away from personal decision to something more external and explanatory that can be discussed and taken issue with.

The problem with traditional praise and reward responses is that they tend to mark the end of the process: 'What level/grade/merit did I get? End of story'. Interactive teachers try to keep the learning going.

Reflection 11.2

Consider how your pupils are praised and rewarded.

Does this kind of feedback seem to motivate them?

Does it divert attention from quality in performance?

My pupils have these ways of being praised and rewarded, with these strengths and weaknesses:

. . . .

. . . .

. . . .

NEXT STEP

Feedback can motivate my pupils more effectively by:

. . . .

. . . .

. . . .

Feeling the buzz

Formative feedback puts impressions and judgements into words. But appraisals involve feelings too, and can be expressed in a smile, a 'Thank-you', a 'Wow', a choice or a change in behaviour. These two secondary school teachers described how vital this kind of communication is:

> *I know that was a good lesson because ___ [boy], who was disaffected last lesson, was making lots of contributions and quite happy to read his work out. And ____ [another boy], who didn't get a level in his SATs [the previous year], was reading out his work, and he'd got the right idea. Perhaps more immediately, any discussion you have at the end about what you've done and what you've learned. There's also that intangible buzz, when you can see everybody's on task and learning, their enthusiasm for the next lesson, how they leave the room. Formally in the plenary, informally classroom buzz.*

I will actually discuss now, not only the tasks, but why we're doing them and what we do. . . . I always try to measure how many of them talk to me when they go out about some history thing that they did. That's my benchmark: do they troop out or do they come up to me and say 'I saw this on the telly the other day' or 'My dad says'? That's always a good one actually. If they say 'My mum or my dad says', it means they've been talking. When you hear those words, you know you've managed something.

Perhaps the important thing here is that it is the pupils themselves who initiate and express their pleasure and pride.

Reflection 11.3

Consider how your pupils show positive feelings about their activities.

My pupils have these ways of showing they appreciate what they are achieving:

. . . .

. . . .

. . . .

NEXT STEP

My pupils can express enjoyment and satisfaction more by:

. . . .

. . . .

. . . .

Recording achievement

The process of appreciating what has been achieved culminates in records of various kinds. These can be attractive collections of pieces of work, mementos and reflections, reviews, reports or certificates.

A special school deputy headteacher described the development her school has undergone:

A major step forward has been in simplifying and making relevant to pupils the way progress is recorded. Records now have to involve, and make sense to, the pupils. Where previously it was possible for pupils to gain accreditation without understanding what their record stated, they now see and contribute to the record, which for each element states the pupil's name, the module and unit, contains photographs and notes on progress and achievement, making use of the pupil's voice. The paper-chase of evidence for accreditation has been abolished, with accreditation now occurring, not continuously, but at Year 11 and Year 13, allowing pupils to get the best they can. Unless the pupil is involved, evidence is not included in the record.

The only statutory requirement in this respect is the annual reporting of progress and achievement to parents. Schools have considerable powers to decide how to record their pupils' experiences and accomplishments.

Reflection 11.4

Check the different ways your pupils have of recording their achievements.

My pupils record their achievements by:

. . . .

. . . .

. . . .

NEXT STEP

My pupils can record their achievements more effectively, and receive more effective recognition, by:

. . . .

. . . .

. . . .

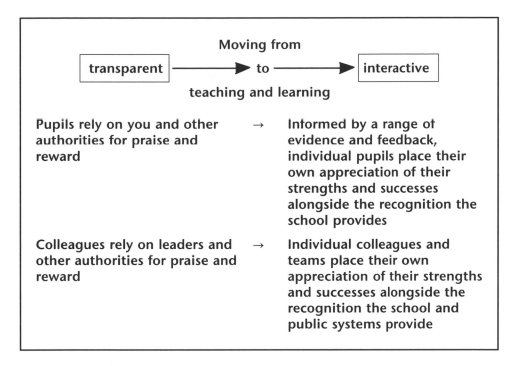

First take account of strengths

It would be nice if policy for assessment kept up with innovative developments in teaching and learning and in the recording and reporting of pupils' progress and achievement. Outstanding formative assessment practices do not sit comfortably with a public emphasis on summatively reported results.

There is public relations work to be done with parents to enable them to understand how the school is developing and why, particularly in relation to marking and rewards. Newsletters, website postings, open days and meetings can help. And the best advocates of effective work are the pupils themselves.

Transparency and interactivity in leadership create opportunities for colleagues to share practice within and across teams. Some develop case studies to use for in-house coaching and training and to inform visitors. Increasingly, the SEF is being used to record achievements in professional development and whole-school improvement. The SEF, together with the SDP, can present innovations and evaluations relating to formative assessment.

Collaborative action research, sometimes supported by external advisers or consultants, promotes this kind of development. An infant school teacher spoke to one of his research facilitators about the year's achievement as part of the AfL project:

> *The interviews have provided an opportunity to sit down and reflect on the process. Speaking to you has made me recall all the things that we have done, and makes me feel positive about it all.*

Under the headteacher's guidance and with a consultant's assistance, the staff of an infant school carried out a whole-school review of AfL. They used *Getting in the Habit* (Johns and Blanchard, 2007), which was one of the resources produced by the Portsmouth project, based on the key questions in 'Ten things to be clear about' (see Appendix 2). The notes below illustrate how recognition of achievement can be used as a platform for further development:

- *AfL already forms part of the school improvement plan (**SIP**).*
- *In the last academic year the staff were given the AfL SEF and asked to highlight areas they felt they were already engaged with. This was followed up with specific staff meetings.*
- *When* Getting in the Habit *arrived in school, it was distributed to staff.*
- *Two staff meetings were then allocated to the document and each key question was considered in turn. The strategies and actions were discussed to see how they fitted with staff perceptions of where the school was.*
- *Having agreed what had been achieved, a decision was then taken as to what development, if any, each key question required.*
- *This information was then collated by the headteacher and added to the SIP.*
- *Priorities were agreed upon, and these formed the basis of the headteacher's monitoring for the term. The priorities were:*
  - *every lesson to have learning objectives and success criteria;*
  - *success criteria to be revisited at the end of each lesson;*
  - *more pupil self assessment throughout lessons;*
  - *writing up learning objectives and success criteria in the classroom would progress through the year.*
- *Individual feedback was given and a whole-school sheet produced on 'Good Practice'.*
- *The next task is to undertake work sampling to check for evidence of regular good practice.*
- *The document has now become an integral part of the SIP. Next priorities are easily highlighted, discussed and actioned.*

These comments were made by the school's headteacher and staff on the use of this resource and process of reviewing AfL:

- *The format was easy to use.*
- *The strategy is in clear, easily understood, language.*
- *There was an absence of jargon.*
- *It acted as a catalyst for discussion.*
- *It lifted spirits as staff could recognize what they had already achieved.*
- *Highlighting led to a focusing on priorities.*
- *Staff were able to have a clear agreement on what would be done by everyone.*
- *It fitted well with AfL being part of the SIP, staff having attended AfL training and the school receiving a day's monitoring by the consultant on AfL practice.*
- *It enabled next priorities to be highlighted and trialled by some staff, before being rolled out across the school.*
- *It made staff aware of the time needed for practice to become embedded.*
- *It enabled staff to focus on engaging the pupils in the process of learning, which is in turn leading to pupils' topic selection.*
- *Staff discussion led to new ideas, such as printing out sticky labels with learning objectives and success criteria on them for each child's book, which in turn led to easier marking against the success criteria, being readily shared and implemented.*

The headteacher commented, as follows, on the benefits of this resource and process, particularly when it came to Ofsted inspection:

- *Primarily it demonstrated the school's use of an external benchmark against which it could judge its own practice, and showed how far 'along the road' we are to becoming an AfL school.*
- *It was a point of discussion between the inspectors and the headteacher about the monitoring of the quality of teaching (they did not ask to see my monitoring file).*
- *Although we had some actions in our SIP already, there were things in* Getting the Habit *that were indicated to the Ofsted team through the use of the document that we hadn't put in our SIP because they are already part of the way we work.*
- *Differentiated work and teachers' use of differentiation has been referred to in the draft report as an observed and improving area, and this is due to the growing awareness of staff regarding AfL.*
- *Planning for higher achievers has been and is an issue for us, and I am sure that the fact that we were engaging with AfL strategies and documents gave the inspection team confidence that we will be able to meet this challenge.*

Reflection 11.5

Check how development is reflected: for you, for your team(s) and for the school as a whole.

Are your improvements well communicated?

Are they acknowledged by other authorities?

We have these ways of recording and publishing our successful AfL developments:

. . . .

. . . .

. . . .

NEXT STEP

We can communicate our achievements in AfL even more effectively by:

. . . .

. . . .

. . . .

12 'How can we improve?'

> **Working on IMPROVEMENT: taking it up a level**
> - Having opportunity and support to make improvements
> - Improving conditions for development

This chapter covers how learners can be enabled to develop their capabilities, and applies the same principles to professional and whole-school development.

Having opportunity and support to make improvements

Giving and receiving feedback enables learners to appreciate what is going well and what can be better. 'Even better if ...' (EBI) mentioned in the previous chapter, is a convenient tag for the 'How to improve?' question. A primary school pupil gave the general principle:

You can see what you've got to change. You know how to make it better.

She was backed up by a junior school pupil:

You need to know what to do the next time.

And another pinpointed the teacher's role:

She needs to know how we are doing, so if there is a problem she can explain.

Feedback can be direct and immediate in the sense that learners observe their performance and review its features. This is done, for example, when learners study displays, watch video clips and hear sound recordings of what they have been doing. Considering firsthand evidence is one of the most powerful means of promoting learning.

Constructive feedback, which is based on explicit criteria and looks toward improvement, can be provided by teachers, assistants, pupils and other audiences and observers. It can be given face-to-face in spoken, or in written, form. Conscientious teachers agree policy and practice for marking and the wider forms of feedback (see Appendix 4).

Learners need opportunities and routines to enable them to build on their first efforts and feedback. One way of doing this is to give pupils time to improve or extend their performance throughout a topic or unit, for example, using learning partners or coaching. Another way is for an early part of some lessons to be an opportunity for pupils to respond to the marking or feedback they are given. Another way is periodically during a topic or unit to return to the plan or progress chart, for example, as shown on a mind-map or learning wall (see Chapter 5), and enable the pupils to use new assessments to improve their performance.

Teachers who engage with AfL see that their pupils need time and support to develop their work. Rather than prescribing one-off teacher-assessed tasks, which leave learners little or no opportunity to improve, transparent and interactive teaching helps pupils to use feedback to advance their learning. This has been one of the most significant effects of teachers' engagement with the theory and practice of assessment for learning. Junior school pupils saw the benefits:

> *When we get our books back, we have time to make improvements or corrections.*

> *We get comments asking us to look again at specific points. The comments are good at pushing you that extra bit further.*

There are issues to be explored about how much marking is productive, and about what kinds of marking really do help. Special attention has to be paid to the time learners need to make use of their feedback. When teachers feel that they have a great deal of curriculum ground to cover, or that they are duty bound above all else to secure good results in tests, they can find it difficult to spare time or energy for learners' consolidation and improvement of their learning. Changing marking practice almost inevitably involves adjusting the pace and structure of lessons. This is something teaching teams can work on together to prevent individual staff members feeling they are out on a limb.

Some teachers find it helpful to give questions or tasks for pupils to work on as follow-up. An infant school pupil described the system in his class:

> *If we get one right she gives it a tick, and if we get one wrong she gives us a little dot to 'check it'.*

What teachers can try to avoid is pupils' ignoring or merely glancing at their feedback. Pupils can have things to do with the comments they get: finding something out; reworking a section; making changes, such as key words or details; and so on. Though there is little wrong with asking pupils to remember something 'next time', it is far better for them to put guidance into practice right away. (See Appendix 4 for information about marking and feedback policy, and Appendix 8 for an example of marking dialogue.)

Self and peer assessments can produce guidance. Primary school pupils said:

> It helps when others mark your work, but only when they have to tell you how to get better, not just what you've done wrong.

> It's important the comments aren't just about spelling. It has to be something we're trying to do, like alliteration, simile or metaphor.

A range of colourful methods and symbols is used to indicate success and points for further attention. Primary school pupils gave these examples:

> LI* means we've achieved the learning intention, and LI↑ means we're nearly there.

> An orange blob means I wasn't sure about the work.

> Tickled pink means that what you have done is right. Green means that you've got to check what you've done and make it better. It means that you get to check your work and see how you can make it better in the future.

The emphasis is on clear criteria, dialogue, recognizing success, making changes and developing work, rather than passively receiving marking. These secondary school teachers gave interesting examples of effective and evolving practice:

> What I ask them to do is to swap books with their neighbour and read it, and with a pencil to tick their favourite part of their friend's work, and if they want to write, in pencil in the margin, why, and squiggly-underline in pencil anything they're not sure of... They've got to look at the two books together and try to figure out the squiggly-underlined bits: 'What are we going to do to put that right before Miss gets hold of it? Are we going to look this up? Are we going to ask for help if we are stuck? Am I going to look in your book to see if I've written the same or differently?'... Pupils telling each other is much more powerful than me telling them...
>
> We hypercorrect... We actually go through and make the corrections and I'm desperately trying to pull away from that and put the onus back onto them... And when it comes to them asking me questions in the lesson, like 'Miss, how do you spell this?', I say 'How do you think?' In fact my first answer every time is

not to give them the answer, but to ask them what they think first. They have then got time – and this is the really crucial bit – to put it right. In the past we have not ever done that. . . . And that's the thing I've highlighted. . .: we have got to slow down. If we are wanting them to improve the quality of their work, we've got to pay it more attention. And we've got to have a whole package in place to make sure that happens. And it is no good leaving out that final step, because we will never see a difference if they are not told to look at their success criteria and make a correction, or ask for help if they're stuck, or do something active to alter their performance. The whole system will fall down if we don't do that final stage. . . That feeds back to the putting the onus on them, 'Take responsibility for taking it in', not the sloping shoulders bit 'It's not my fault'. . . . This is a way of trying to transmit that to them, and for them to take it in and learn from it. So that they become more independent.

If I take books home, I have failed. I feel I need to have the pupils there, and what we're trying to get them to do is more and more peer assessment. . . . We use an extensive questionnaire with the pupils to monitor how well it's going. There was a complete spectrum of confidence with the pupils about their engagement in this marking process: from some who could see the merit and enjoyed it, and some who were not confident about what their peers were saying. . . The main thing is the work they do afterwards in analysing the strands: 'Am I good at data analysis? If not, what am I going to do about it? Am I good at any particular segment, such as chemistry? Have I a problem there, and if so where am I going to go and get help?' That's something we are building in as a two-way thing, with pupils actually looking at their targets and setting big and little targets: globally in terms of levels, but also related to handwriting and presentation and so on. That is something we have been engaged in for some considerable time now.

The smaller the gap between the giving of feedback and learners acting on it, the better. And one way of confirming, refining and extending what they know is for learners to teach someone else. Articulating and rehearsing capability are opportunities to consolidate and even develop what has been learned.

Reflection 12.1

Check the ways your pupils have to learn beyond their first effort. How do you make time for them to use feedback?

Review your marking policy, for example, using a comparison with another school or a guideline such as the one given in Appendix 4.

My pupils have these ways of improving their performance:

. . . .

. . . .

. . . .

NEXT STEP

My pupils can learn better how to improve their work by:

. . . .

. . . .

. . . .

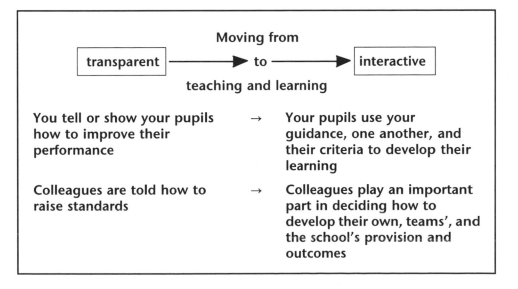

Moving from

| transparent | ——→ to ——→ | interactive |

teaching and learning

You tell or show your pupils how to improve their performance	→	Your pupils use your guidance, one another, and their criteria to develop their learning
Colleagues are told how to raise standards	→	Colleagues play an important part in deciding how to develop their own, teams', and the school's provision and outcomes

Improving conditions for development

There are parallels between pupils' learning in lessons and professionals' development and contribution to whole-school improvement. For example, leaders and staff members can deliberately consolidate and rework changes, rather than feel obliged always to move on to a new imperative or tick the next box in the improvement plan.

Pupils' perceptions are a vital source of feedback (see Appendix 6). A primary school teacher, typical of colleagues engaged in action research, said:

> *What pupils have told me about my marking has changed my approach.*

Genuine and lasting improvement takes time, and it seems to help that this is confidently acknowledged. A junior school teacher made the point:

> *I don't think we shall ever get there completely.*

Leaders have a vital role. Knowing when to give a prompt or support, and when to step back, are part of this. Facilitation involves the framing of auditing processes, collaborative action research, the sustaining of commitment, and rigorous evaluation.

This secondary school senior leader summarized staff members' review of AfL across the school, based on systematic lesson observation. This was what they agreed:

Things that help learning
- *Tasks chunked so pupils break regularly*
- *Pupils discuss how they have learnt*
- *Pupils evaluate what they have learnt*
- *Pupils responsible for their own learning by devising their own tasks*
- *Teacher makes sure pupils understood criteria*
- *Pupils involved in forming their own success criteria*
- *TA monitors and helps*
- *Class asks questions at the end to focus the pupils*
- *The least motivated act as scribe to focus them*
- *Incentive sheets*
- *Seating plans*
- *Praise for good behaviour*
- *Pupils enjoy task and so learn better*
- *Pupils listen to each other more than the teacher*
- *Pupils concentrate more if they know it's for a short period of time*
- *Pupils know where they are and what they need to do to improve.*

Things you are going to try

- *Use 'guided group' as a focus during independent tasks*
- *Devise more fun extension activities as reward for getting through main task*
- *Give pupils more choice about activities*
- *Let pupils do more of whole-class talk*
- *Use small group work more often*
- *Use team games to involve all pupils*
- *Devise incentive sheets*
- *Think about seating more carefully*
- *Involve pupils in devising success criteria*
- *Make learning outcomes more explicit*
- *Test pupils' understanding of criteria, rather than just refer to them and assume they've got it*
- *Vary activities*
- *Less teacher talk.*

The teachers were able to re-visit that list and check their progress. Keeping records of plans, projects and evaluations is essential, enabling everyone to see developments. Appreciating how far individuals, teams and the school have come gives strength to continue the long journey.

Reflection 12.2

Think about when you have improved your practice as a result of:

- working closely with colleagues;
- studying pupils' perceptions and feedback;
- reviewing policies.

Try to identify what made a difference.

These factors and processes have promoted and supported professional and whole-school development in the past:

. . . .

. . . .

. . . .

NEXT STEP

We can give our efforts to improve our teaching, learning and assessment a better chance by:

. . . .

. . . .

. . . .

13 'How can we use what we learn?'

> **Working on APPLICATION: using what we learn**
> - Cross-curricular learning and relevance to life
> - Transfer and cross-fertilization in development

This chapter covers how learners can be helped to apply what they learn in different contexts. The principles that inform teaching and learning in lessons are seen to relate also to professional and whole-school development.

Cross-curricular learning and relevance to life

Some teachers want their pupils to do more than acquire knowledge, understanding and skill in order to pass tests. They don't undervalue summative outcomes or qualifications. But they want their pupils to be able to apply what they learn when they need or want to.

When the outcome of education appears to be a test score, level or grade, it is not easy to emphasize the value of applying learning in real life. But it can be done via shared planning and cross-curricular projects which focus on generic skills and capabilities. Learners can be helped to see overlaps between lesson activities and real-life issues and situations.

Realizing there is practical and lasting value in what they are learning helps pupils succeed here and now *and* do well in tests and examinations. Just learning how to satisfy summative assessment requirements does not help them connect the knowledge and skill they acquire with living contexts.

A Year 4 pupil reflected, for example, on the value of doing peer assessment:

> *When you grow up and work in an office, you will be doing lots of peer assessment.*

A secondary school teacher summed it up:

> *The biggest quantum leap they can make is taking an abstract principle and applying it to other areas.*

The first context for pupils' transfer of their learning is within and between lessons. A secondary modern foreign languages teacher explained:

> It's whether they can take elements of those phrases and apply them to a new situation... a new context, applying 'I went swimming' to 'I made my bed', seeing there's the same structure there that they can lift... I have devised many stepped activities, taking it from a reading to a matching exercise, to a complete-half-a-sentence, to a now-do-one-completely-independently... We do expect them to think, to make links, to apply.

Applying what they know in tests and examinations can be a step toward seeing the relevance to life, if this is talked about in lessons. The learning can involve making connections between different lessons, between lessons and test requirements, and between lessons and activities in private study, leisure and employment. A sixth form teacher saw it like this:

> It's all about applying what they've been learning to any problem they may be given in the examination. They have to learn how to evaluate (using concepts of 'cultural bias', 'ethnocentrism', 'ecological validity', 'internal validity', 'relia-bility' and 'ethics'), and use those in contexts of their own choosing, whether that be the environment, health, crime, sport or education.

And her students discussed as a group how they might use what they had learned during Year 12, not only in the subject of psychology, but across all their subjects and in the future:

- *I need good regular attendance.*
- *If I work hard, I can excel.*
- *You have to apply the discipline of DEFINITION, POINT, EVIDENCE, EXAMPLES.*
- *I have to revise.*
- *I revise well when I get a reward at the end of it.*
- *Not to judge myself negatively: to see what I have achieved.*
- *I can be less narrow-minded, more open-minded.*
- *Don't take anything for granted.*
- *Once I've been taught evaluative skills, it becomes a habit to apply them.*
- *It helps me learn when I teach someone else what I've learned.*
- *My best way to learn is in a small study group.*
- *I learn best by making my own flashcards.*
- *I need motivation and organization.*
- *You've got to have willpower.*
- *You have to make sacrifices to succeed.*
- *You have to plan well to cope with the pressure.*

- *I can apply problem-solving to career interviews, etc.*
- *I can apply the skills I learn in psychology to other subjects.*
- *A-level is a real jump from GCSE.*

Often there are those two sorts of answer to the question 'What is this learning for?' One answer relates to tests and qualifications, the other to qualities and capabilities that are likely to serve pupils well in their lives, now and in the future. An interesting aspect of teachers' engagement with AfL is their coming to terms with questions about why they teach what they teach.

Effective and interactive teachers arrange time and support for their pupils to apply what they learn in new and different contexts. One way of doing that is to enable pupils to coach one another. Another is to give pupils opportunities to plan and pursue their own projects and interests.

An infant school's senior leaders summarized the learning that their pupils were increasingly able to apply across the school and beyond:

Our pupils:
- *are becoming independent in their use of routines, such as fetching equipment and materials, and are supported in this by posters and displays;*
- *are enabled to share their work with others, to help and be helped by one another;*
- *are helped to build on existing and recently acquired knowledge, skill and understanding;*
- *are enabled to see their work in terms of what they can do and in terms of how they can improve it;*
- *use clear criteria that are displayed and referred to;*
- *use feedback referring explicitly to criteria;*
- *find a suitable way into tasks that match developmental need;*

with benefits such as they:
- *take responsibility for what they do;*
- *develop confidence and cooperation;*
- *have opportunities to rehearse, reinforce and extend their learning;*

evidenced by:
- *pupils' responses to the activities they are asked to tackle;*
- *pupils' performance;*
- *teachers' and teaching assistants' assessments of pupils' progress.*

These secondary school pupils discussed as a group how what they were learning through AfL and Student Voice was having important benefits:

It helps with confidence...

I can now speak out and make myself heard, and I couldn't before...

I've known her for years, and used to go to junior school with her. She was a timid sort of girl, like sit-down-timid-quiet-hide-behind-her-hair-wouldn't-say-anything kind of girl.

It's good for teaching you skills that you can use in the future, like multi-tasking...

You also get respect from it. It makes you feel a better person because you've really helped someone else, and helped your group and your school.

In these ways learners develop good answers to their questions 'Why are we doing this? What is the point of learning this?'

Reflection 13.1

Consider ways in which you enable your pupils to relate what they are learning in lessons to other areas of study and aspects of life outside school.

My pupils are helped to make connections between subjects, and with real-life matters, by:

. . . .

. . . .

. . . .

NEXT STEP

Our pupils can learn more about transferring and applying their learning by:

. . . .

. . . .

. . . .

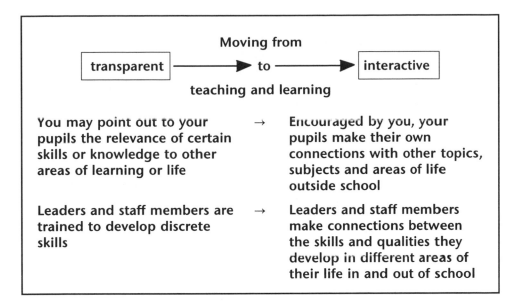

Transfer and cross-fertilization in development

Conscientious leaders and teachers want to develop what they do so that the whole institution benefits as well as their own area of work. While respecting subject differences, effort can go into seeking common ground in values and approaches. Effective development focuses on agreeing principles, while allowing for diversity in concrete specifics.

Here is an example. The staffs of an infant school and a junior school expected their schools to amalgamate at some point in the future. They spent two staff meetings reviewing their work on AfL. The purpose was to increase collaboration, consistency and progression across the two schools. This gave a genuine reason and context for transferring and applying what they had learned about AfL. They made this statement:

- *Assessment depends on good modelling and a constructive ethos.*
- *Learning criteria may relate to a lesson or a week's learning or longer.*
- *Formal feedback (marking) is not given for every piece of work.*
- *Feedback focuses on task-specific criteria, though some comments may relate to ongoing or overall objectives (such as handwriting and routine skills).*
- *Feedback confirms success and focuses improvement, e.g. via colour coding.*
- *The overall effect of feedback for the pupil is positive, encouraging and helpful.*
- *Sometimes, perhaps more often than not, the pupils have something to do with the feedback they receive.*

- *The methods that we use for giving feedback are such that they are familiar enough to be supportive for the pupils, without becoming dull or offputting; our methods are flexible enough to leave us scope for taking a fresh approach.*
- *The ultimate goal is for pupils to:*
  - *understand their learning criteria;*
  - *adapt and create their own criteria;*
  - *mark their own and one another's work.*

Another example is provided by this secondary school senior leader. He highlighted peer coaching and mentoring as particularly productive ways of enabling colleagues to extend and apply their learning. As a review of his school's achievement in AfL, he made this statement, so that lessons could be applied across the board and into the future:

- *The work was focused by the Ofsted inspection judgement that in some lessons the students were not encouraged to take a full and active part.*
- *Small scale piloting has been used to support innovative work and promote dissemination of good practice by staff across the school.*
- *The work has had continuity and has avoided the one-off-initiatives syndrome.*
- *A school improvement group, the school development plan, and departmental agendas and plans have been linked and made coherent.*
- *Other schools have joined in INSET sessions.*
- *Quality INSET, provided by a respected consultant and trainer, launched the process.*
- *Time for consolidation is vital, as is keeping it fresh, so this has been kept at the forefront of thinking.*
- *The decision was taken to ask staff who had trialled certain strategies 'Can you run a session for colleagues?'*
- *The emphasis has been on openness about teaching at all levels, e.g. deputy head is observed by colleagues teaching a consolidation lesson.*
- *Keynotes have been ENGAGE WITH RESEARCH and SHARE.*
- *Evidence of AfL's benefits are:*
  - *a rising trend in standards;*
  - *work sampling showing effective feedback and responses;*
  - *success for the majority of pupils in the mentoring scheme.*
- *We are aware that it is still early days for some aspects, such as self and peer assessment and pupils using written feedback.*

Reflection 13.2

Consider the opportunities your senior leaders and staff members have of applying what they learn in one context to other areas of their work.

We have these ways of transferring our skills and expertise from one context to another:

. . . .

. . . .

. . . .

NEXT STEP

We can develop our capacity to transfer and apply what we learn about teaching, learning and assessment by:

. . . .

. . . .

. . . .

14 Whole-school and continuing professional development

Basing improvement on PRINCIPLES and PRAGMATISM

- Matching means and ends; matching individual and collective aims
- Committing to long-term, sustainable development
- Paired and team working
- Learning from self evaluations, from pupils' and others' views
- Reporting progress and achievement
- Strategies for developing whole-school assessment for learning

This chapter brings together ideas and strategies for continuing professional development allied with whole-school improvement. It answers the question: How can formative assessment be implemented and embedded across a school?

Matching means and ends; matching individual and collective aims

Teachers as well as leaders can feel under pressure to get results and see this as being in conflict with reflection and innovation. Far-sighted leadership makes clear that its aims for pupils' learning have to be lived out in the way professional and whole-school development is conducted. Coherence of methods and objectives is a hallmark of outstanding institutions.

An infant school headteacher spoke about this:

> In the appointment of new staff, dispositions and attitudes are crucial... With the children we want a culture of being prepared to make a mistake.

Shared values lead to professionals as well as pupils knowing what to expect. These primary school teachers saw consistency of practice as important and beneficial:

> There is now a greater continuity of experience for pupils due to the dissemination of the work to other staff as they move from one lesson to another.

> The whole school is now sharing learning intentions and success criteria with their classes and in their planning.

Next year the teacher receiving my children will know that they are used to discussing success criteria and marking each others' work.

*AfL is as important in **PE** as it is in English.*

*Learning intentions are shared with the **LSA**s [learning support assistants), and it is intended that this work be disseminated to them via the SENCo. It is recognized that consistency of message across the school is required, e.g. LSAs need to be aware of wait-time rather than encouraging pupils to put their hands up and appear eager to answer.*

This does not have to mean uniformity of practice. When everyone subscribes to the agreed principles, there is scope for individual talents, styles and preferences. A primary school headteacher explained:

*It is our whole-school policy to state a learning intention for all lessons, but how this is done is left to the discretion of the staff, for example methods such as **WALT** [We Are Learning To ...] being more appropriate for use with younger children.*

Such tolerance of individuality seems to be associated with leadership's assertiveness and proactivity. An infant school teacher put it like this:

We're changing school culture from 'done unto' towards taking responsibility for teaching and learning.

Pupils too can be shrewd commentators on all of this. These Year 9 pupils reflected on the significance of the work they did to redesign part of the religious education curriculum for Key Stage 3:

Here you've got such trust and such connection with the teachers... We were looking at what would work with the teachers and the pupils: a way that teachers could teach their lessons and a way that the pupils would actually be able to learn and be interested throughout the lesson. So we were being the kind of link between the pupils and the teachers.

Teachers can take learners' views into account, and leaders can take staff members' views into account. It is a vital function of leadership to encourage confidence in the needs and aspirations of the individuals who make up local communities. These are sources of motivation and direction for development. The better the representation of interested parties in processes of research, discussion and decision-making, the better for everyone will be the experience of working toward shared goals.

Institutional change reflects the journeys that everyone makes. Leadership draws boundaries, points the way and sets an example.

Reflection 14.1

Check how closely your construction of development opportunities and processes reflects the learning you want to promote in lessons.

We seek integrity between our aims and methods of development by:

. . . .

. . . .

. . . .

NEXT STEP

We can bring greater integrity to our efforts to develop teaching, learning and assessment by:

. . . .

. . . .

. . . .

Committing to long-term, sustainable development

The principles and practices of formative assessment can become part of a school's culture. This junior school teacher felt her school was achieving this:

AfL is just part of what we do!

There are no ready-made solutions in teaching or in leadership: the problems are always peculiar to their context. Effective development depends on recognizing the strengths of existing practice, and using the best that research has to offer to point the way forward. Leaders and teachers can take notice of what professional and academic bodies report, and carry out their own action research. All of this takes time and determination.

A junior school deputy headteacher knew:

If someone expects an overnight change in a school that is on the assessment for learning journey, then they will be disappointed. Assessment for learning requires a fundamental change in behaviour of teachers and a shift in their perceptions and attitudes, and these radical notions take time.

Reflection 14.2

Consider the view you and your colleagues take about change. What kind of development are you interested in? How long will it take?

This is how we see change: as individuals, in our teams, and as a school:

. . . .

. . . .

. . . .

NEXT STEP

We can develop our approach to development by:

. . . .

. . . .

. . . .

Paired and team working

Fellow professionals are their own most accessible source of example, advice and challenge. A secondary school teacher said:

I think that quality work with a couple of other members of committed staff who you work with and who become advocates through their own experience is the way in which you will change schools slowly. I think that anything imposed – too big, grand in scale – is doomed to failure.

It was noticeable that many of our teachers acknowledged how much they learn from their colleagues. A primary school teacher commented:

> *What's become interesting is that, by doing these AfL strategies, it has increased the amount of professional dialogue within the school, between teachers... There's been a whole culture of expertise sharing.*

We found certain activities indispensable to the progress that our schools made with formative assessment. Commonest and most striking were joint practice in planning, teaching and reviewing, accompanied by supportive and challenging observation. These generated reflective practice *and* accountability.

Sustainable development depends on working partnerships across the school. Colleagues can be enabled to be open with one another about their aspirations, anxieties and achievements. Shared planning, peer observation, coaching and mentoring are ways of making collaboration concrete and focused. They create a virtuous circle of pride and a desire to do the very best.

Some schools find colleagues' peer coaching invaluable. Teachers and assistants can observe, support and feed back to one another, reviewing strengths and choosing possible areas for development. Some schools make a distinction for the pupils between talk partners and critical friends (see Chapter 4 page 30), and carry this over to the adults. Accordingly, a coach is an observer and commentator, focusing on the individual's own agenda; a mentor is a critic and adviser, focusing on public standards.

Colleagues observing one another's lessons has become a major force for development in some schools. Here is my summary account of one experience:

> *The leaders and staff of a special school invited a headteacher in another local authority and me to observe a range of lessons over two days. The project was designed to set up a system of teachers' peer observation and feedback throughout the whole school. For each observation we were accompanied by a host-colleague so that they could learn about the process and trial it for themselves. The headteacher and I led each feedback meeting, but as soon as possible handed initiative over to the teachers. There was a real sense of commitment, enthusiasm and shared learning. The school reported a year later that peer observation and review were well established as an essential element in professional dialogue and whole-school development.*

Colleagues benefit from partners in development and small teams trying out and sharing ideas. Innovations and solutions can be talked through and reflected on. Teachers appreciate collaborators rather than inspectors.

A primary school teacher described her experience:

> *The process has been like a professional dialogue. It has been beneficial to talk about what is going on and what has been difficult.*

Teachers who trial new methods and take a lead in action research can go on to provide in-service training for their colleagues. A secondary school deputy headteacher explained:

> *I have been so impressed with the SIG* [school improvement group] *as a group of staff. This is the fifth school I've worked in and I've never come across a group like it. They're a very proactive group of people, who actually want to see something happen... It's 'Let's enhance everybody's practice'. It's a powerful motivator and a really crucial factor in where AfL is at in our school at the moment. I think if that group didn't exist, we'd be nowhere near where we are at the moment with AfL a key component in the vast majority of classrooms to support the learning... We've had members of the SIG leading INSET for the whole of the staff that was all positively received, and actually we've had staff saying 'Are you going to be running those sessions again?' ... What really pleases me is the way that staff are proud of their practice and confident in sharing that practice with other members of staff. That is a move forward because of the climate of 'It's coming from you'.*

Reflection 14.3

Consider how colleagues are enabled to share their work with one another and inspire one another.

We have these ways of learning from one another:

. . . .

. . . .

. . . .

NEXT STEP

We can make better use of one another's strengths and expertise by:

. . . .

. . . .

. . . .

Learning from self evaluations, from pupils' and others' views

An infant school teacher was clear about how working together increases awareness of achievement:

> *Discussing and sharing our work makes us realize how much we have done.*

Seeing things through another's eyes and seeing how others do things can have a powerful effect on rethinking what is possible, what is desirable, even what is necessary. These two secondary school teachers valued learning directly from colleagues outside their own school, including the primary phase:

> *It's very important to see practice in other schools, that kind of pollination. Because every five minutes you spend talking to a colleague in a different school where you bring something back, and something changes, that's more valuable than INSET. You don't sit there passively and absorb great ideas. You see them and you get enthused by them.*

> *What worried me when we were at _____ Junior School was that I had no idea that their AfL was so advanced. They've got the three levels of challenge; they're using the traffic lights; WALT and WILF are just part of their everyday language. They come to secondary school, and it's like going back five or six years. Unless people realize that, the pupils are going to get even more disillusioned, and that dip's going to get even bigger.*

It is also invaluable for all members of staff to have access to pupils' perceptions and feelings about lessons and school (see Appendix 6). Sometimes senior leaders carry out interviews, group discussions and surveys, but do not enable staff members to have the same experience. It weakens whole-school understanding of, and commitment to, areas of development if this kind of information is 'handed down'.

A powerful way of enabling senior leaders and staff members to learn about their own and other schools' provision is to arrange 'learning walks', that is, focused visits to lessons and other areas of school life. Even more powerful is arranging for pupils to do the same, so that they can make recommendations, based on what they like about how things are done in the school/s they visit. These are notes on my participation in a project whereby secondary schools set up pupils' three-way exchange visits:

> *Each of three schools arranged for twelve Year 9 pupils to visit and host visits from the other two schools. The pupils organized tours and participation in*

lessons during the morning. Then a senior teacher lightly chaired a meeting of all the pupils, so that perceptions could be shared. The outcome was that each pupil team decided what they wanted to take away from the school they visited as recommendations for improvement back in their own school. A group of pupils made a presentation to senior leadership and staff about what they had learned and how they'd like to see their school develop.

Development can also be supported by outsiders, acting in a supportive yet challenging role for individuals, teams and/or the school. These two infant school teachers saw strengths in their collaborative action research with project partners who carried out interviews and wrote up reports:

The interviews have provided an opportunity to sit down and reflect on the process. Speaking to you has made me recall all the things that we have done and makes me feel positive about it all.

Ongoing contact would be very useful. A visit every six months to discuss developments and progress would help to maintain focus.

This junior school teacher, having received her visiting researcher's draft report, responded:

I enjoyed reading it and enjoyed commenting on it. Thank you. . . It helps me see with another pair of eyes! I'm glad you found it worthwhile too. Thanks for coming and fitting in so flexibly.

PS We did OK in our Ofsted visit. . . although, of course, we have things to work on to improve. That's life for everyone isn't it. . . . the continual improvement cycle.

Reflection 14.4

Consider how colleagues and pupils currently comment on the quality of what happens in lessons and other areas of school life.

We have these ways of learning from our colleagues' and pupils' perceptions:

. . . .

. . . .

. . . .

Consider how colleagues and pupils currently learn about how other schools do things, so that different approaches are suggested and explored.

We have these ways of learning from colleagues' and pupils' perceptions elsewhere:

. . . .

. . . .

. . . .

NEXT STEP

We can make better use of colleagues' and pupils' views, here and elsewhere, by:

. . . .

. . . .

. . . .

Reporting progress and achievement

From time to time, colleagues can sum up what they have been aiming for and what they have so far achieved. Reviews serve to:

- spread and spur on development;
- present a confident view of school development;
- promote discussion.

Here are some examples. A junior school headteacher summarized:

AfL will survive. It was a life-changing set of ideas, and now it is evolving. Teachers are taking it on as their own. It is part of good and outstanding teaching and learning. The pupils are more active in their learning. AfL takes different forms and the pupils are devising their own strategies now.

A primary school deputy headteacher gave a progress report:

The assessment for learning practices have enabled the children to take control of their learning and made them more independent.

A primary school teacher reported:

As a result of using learning intentions and success criteria children have become better at answering questions specifically and being able to justify their answers: their explanatory skills are being developed. The confidence of the children has increased: they are now happy to show when they don't understand or are unsure, and can explain the difficulty.

A junior school teacher's analysis was:

What works most?
- *the success criteria ('Remember to . . .');*
- *simplifying the aim;*
- *involving the pupils;*
- *making them think;*
- *getting them to share their work with one another;*
- *'the big picture' – at the beginning of the work we look at what we're going to be doing, and going through that clearly;*
- *at the beginning of a session, asking 'What did we do yesterday?';*
- *finding out what we already know about the topic;*
- *emphasizing that 'The whole point is that the work makes sense to you';*
- *emphasizing that 'What we do is help you';*
- *using the 'Remember to . . .' points to tick off what has been achieved as we go along;*
- *using an envelope for the pupils to write questions they have.*

And a junior school deputy headteacher identified these main features in his school's development:

- *ongoing assessment;*
- *talking with the pupils about their aim and points to remember, because talking is best;*
- *using the points to remember throughout the lesson, not just at the beginning and at the end.*

Reflection 14.5

Consider how well your professional and whole-school development is represented in teams' reviews and plans, reports to governors, your school self evaluation, and other channels of communication.

We have these ways of reporting evaluations:

. . . .

. . . .

. . . .

NEXT STEP

We can more effectively report our developments in teaching, learning and assessment by:

. . . .

. . . .

. . . .

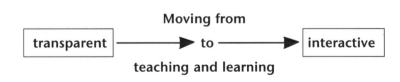

Moving from

| transparent | ➤ to ➤ | interactive |

teaching and learning

| Senior leaders decide the school's vision and plan for improvement | → | Staff members have a role in deciding individual as well as whole-school aims and ways of developing |
| Everyone relies on other authorities to tell them how well or how badly they are doing | → | Everyone enjoys playing a part in describing and documenting the school's strengths and successes |

See Appendix 9 for examples of whole-school development.

Finally here are some practical suggestions about what you can do to develop and evaluate formative assessment across your school.

Strategies for developing whole-school assessment for learning

Policy moves

- Revise your whole-school assessment policy so that it highlights AfL in lessons.
- Introduce a policy whereby different areas of the school (e.g. subjects, PSHE, tutorial and pastoral work, mentoring, SEN ...) have ways of sharing and disseminating their practices and developments.

Assigning roles

- Have an AfL co-ordinator who stimulates and collects accounts of developments across the school, who links with colleagues from other schools and centres, who reports your experience and brings different ideas into your school or centre.
- Have a group to lead AfL development and reflection: e.g. representing different subjects, year teams, with different levels of seniority including subject leaders, newly qualified teachers, trainee teachers, etc.
- Have advanced skills teachers (**ASTs**), perhaps working across a pair or small group of schools, lead trials and dissemination of interesting practice.
- Have teachers initiate experiments in AfL, report to the staff and lead development across the school.
- Have subject areas focus on specific AfL strategies, for example, deliberately covering a range of strategies or the same one or two strategies.
- Have pupils as researchers explore and report on AfL.

Changing procedures for planning, monitoring, evaluating and reporting

- Prioritize AfL in school improvement planning and activity.
- Link AfL with other initiatives, such as 'creativity', pupil voice, personalized learning, SEAL, citizenship and inclusion.
- Make AfL a regular focus in training sessions, staff meetings and team meetings.

- Use senior leaders', teachers' and classroom assistants' performance management reviews and objectives to highlight AfL.
- Make AfL a focus of parent interviewing and questionnairing.
- Make AfL a focus of pupil interviewing and questionnairing.
- Use reports to parents to communicate pupils' achievements through AfL.
- Have subject leaders report to senior management on AfL development in their annual subject reviewing.
- Make films of AfL in practice.
- Make AfL developments a focus of intranet and website communication.
- Make portfolios of pupils' assessed work, including notes on the role of AfL in their teaching and learning (see Appendix 5).
- Make AfL a thread running through your self evaluation reports.

Working with and learning from others

- Invite other schools and centres to share your AfL policy and practice, and explore theirs.
- Share AfL experiences with schools and education providers from which your pupils come and to which they graduate.
- Encourage the governing body to focus on AfL in visits and take a special interest in AfL.
- Invite outsiders such as university researchers, LA consultants and/or Ofsted inspectors to comment on AfL in the school.

Strategies

- Use a list of AfL techniques as an in-service training starter, e.g. 'Assessment for Learning – Reviewing current practice' (Appendix 1), indicating which techniques are used regularly/occasionally/never.
- Use the 'Ten things to be aware of' (Appendix 2) as a framework for reflective practice in whole-school improvement. Choose one or two as an initial focus, e.g. one strength to build on and one of the ten as an area for development.
- Clarify criteria for the school's development of AfL: what will successful and effective AfL look like across the school in one year, in three years? Revisit and update your criteria in the light of experience after one year, two years, etc.

Taking action to develop whole-school provision is more effective when it is rigorously evaluated. The questions below address how well your structures and systems promote development, and point up lessons for future work.

Processes

- How well have teachers and teaching assistants been trained to reflect on and change their practices?
- How well have new practices been introduced in the classroom?
- How well have the leadership and management prepared and supported changes in policy and practice?
- How well have outside-school agencies supported the introduction of revised practices?
- How well are revised practices being monitored and evaluated?

Perceptions

- What do pupils think of AfL developments?
- What do staff members think of AfL developments?
- What do leaders think of AfL developments?
- How do other stakeholders think of AfL developments?

Effects

- What difference have changes to policy and practice made to staff members' and leaders' attitudes?
- What difference have revised practices made to pupils' attitudes and behaviour?
- What difference have revised practices made to value-added measures of pupils' attainment?
- How well have revised practices contributed to the school's capacity to plan, carry out and evaluate its own development?

The following is a format for recording plans and progress:

Whole-school development of formative assessment

Planning and reviewing dates:

Aims

Benefits

Evidence

Evaluation activities

Next steps

15 Formative *versus* summative assessment

- Why it is helpful to be deliberate about learning
- Conflicting purposes, processes and products in assessment
- Implications for policy

This chapter shows how summative assessment detracts from the kinds of learning that formative assessment promotes. It answers the questions:

- How do formative and summative assessments differ?
- What are the implications for policy?

The arguments made here apply as much to adults as they do to young learners. What is true of the part teachers can play in lessons is true also of the part leaders can play in professional and institutional development.

Why it is helpful to be deliberate about learning

Activity is the minimum that you want from your pupils. Activity is the involuntary or deliberate performance of knowledge, understanding and skill:

$$(capability) \times (performance) = activity$$

$$(lesson) - (activity) = O$$

We say pupils are on or off task, 'engaged in activity' or not. But we might reserve the notion of engagement for something more than pupils being occupied in legitimate or prescribed activity. Engagement signals involvement and commitment.

The ingredient that turns activity into engagement is interest. When pupils are interested in what they do, they are more than occupied:

$$(activity) + (interest) = engagement$$

As a teacher you would rather your pupils be active than idle or passive. You would rather they be interested than bored or indifferent. Your aim can be that they be engaged.

Interests range from fleeting tastes and short-lived preferences to abiding preoccupations and profound determinants of well-being. When you take your pupils' interests seriously, they trust you. The more serious their interests, the greater the trust. If you want to enable your pupils to learn things that really mean something to them, you build their trust by acting on their interests.

Ultimately you want your pupils to be more than busy, even with things that interest them: you want them to learn. Learning is more than the involuntary or deliberate performance of knowledge, understanding and skill. Learning is the involuntary or deliberate development of activity:

$$(\text{activity}) \times (\text{development}) = \text{learning}$$

You value engagement because it promises greater ownership of learning than obedient or rote behaviour. The reward is a growing sense of self worth and eagerness to learn more:

$$(\text{learning}) \times (\text{engagement}) = \text{confidence}$$

What someone does can be plainer to see than what someone learns. Learning has to be interpreted or attributed, and this is one of the functions of assessment. You can be aware of what your pupils learn, and you can communicate this to them, as they prepare, as they work, as they reflect on what they do and learn.

Praising your pupils' learning belongs to transparent teaching. But you can do better than this. You can enable your pupils to appreciate for themselves what they learn. They can outgrow dependence on your estimation.

Your pupils see for themselves what they learn in two ways. First, they realize their learning as enhanced capability: *I now know this*. Then your pupils realize their learning as applied capability: *Let's see how I can use what I know*. Recognizing their learning gives pupils a sense of satisfaction, purpose, and potential to learn more. This awareness translates into enhanced capacity to formulate intentions and pursue goals:

$$(\text{confidence}) \times (\text{awareness}) = \text{autonomy}$$

Autonomy does not mean absolute or anarchic self-determination. To be autonomous, or to be in the process of developing autonomy, means finding it safe and rewarding to act on one's own needs, wants and interests in contexts that inevitably entail limiting as well as facilitating factors. Limitations on achievement exist within as well as outside the learner.

Autonomy is not unbounded freedom. It brings the individual into negotiation with others. For pupils, this means dealing with authorities' duties. For professionals, it means accommodating statutory and public requirements.

> The goal of autonomy turns transparent assessment and education into interactive assessment and education: the learner becomes a partner with, and even guide to, the teacher, co-determining purposes, criteria and outcomes. As long as the teacher controls and carries out assessment, however formatively, it can be no more than transparent. When the learner joins the teacher in making assessments, the experience becomes interactive, and greater autonomy follows.

Conflicting purposes, processes and products in assessment

Formative and summative assessments differ in their treatment of activity, engagement, learning, confidence and autonomy.

Summative assessment treats abilities as though they were finite and absolute: it tries to hold them still. Formative assessment accepts that abilities can develop and change: it expects them to change. Summative assessment succeeds when it defines the limits of learners' capabilities. Formative assessment succeeds when learners advance.

Summative assessment is the making of judgements about how well pupils have learned what they should have been taught. Summative assessment treats performance as a valid, reliable indicator of completed, measurable or describable learning. Most commonly this is done by means of tests or examinations. But summative assessments can also be made by means of informal observations, conversations, and surveying written output, artefacts and recorded performance. Summative assessors apply authorized criteria.

The results often take the form of a level, grade, score or percentage, but summative assessments might equally produce a verbal account. When a teacher says 'They can't test a hypothesis', 'They show empathy', or 'They just about know the four rules', a summative assessment is made, whether or not it is recorded or published. When reported, classified performance testifies to the use of sanctioned criteria.

Formative assessment is the making of judgements about how to take pupils' learning forward. Often it results in modified behaviour rather than a mental or recorded note: teachers, assistants and/or pupils decide what to do. There is no need to dwell on classification or monitor how criteria are applied.

Summative assessment takes for granted learners' commitment to passing their examination. Formative assessment seeks to enrich the learners' commitment to curriculum activity as an intrinsically enjoyable experience and catalyst for further learning.

Summative assessment informs third parties, such as parents, teachers at the next stage, prospective trainers and employers, as well as the learners themselves and their teachers. It overlooks progress in favour of attainment. It is concerned with products, not processes, of learning. It restricts examinees' means of expression and the indicators available to assessors. It spotlights competences thought to be creditable. It avoids capabilities that seem difficult to pin down. It values what can be measured or succinctly described.

A.V. Kelly's (1992: 4) caution is worth citing:

> Accuracy of assessment is related inversely to the complexity and the sophistication of what is being assessed. And, since education is a highly complex and sophisticated process, educational assessment can be regarded as measurement only in the remotest of metaphorical senses.

The outcome of summative assessment should be dependable qualification. The outcome of formative assessment should be learning. In each case, the result may be enhanced by learners' understanding the criteria that apply.

In summative assessment understanding their criteria informs examinees' demonstration of specified skill and knowledge. In formative assessment understanding their criteria benefits learners' growing capability and autonomy.

Traditional summative assessment is norm-referenced, designed to select individuals for education, employment or promotion. Candidates are ranked, and cut-offs made, according to the number of places available. A bell curve, or curve of normal distribution, can be drawn. Criteria may remain implicit, because it is the rank order or the banding that matters. Norm-referencing seems to reflect competition in society: one person's success is at the expense of another's. The focus is on the elite.

In the late 1980s educational testing, responding in the United Kingdom to the TGAT Report (DES, 1987), shifted towards criterion-referencing. This uses explicit criteria to define valued attributes, an example being the English national curriculum's level descriptions. There seems to be greater openness about criteria when there is greater access to opportunity. Everyone competes against pre-determined standards, rather than against other people. The focus is on qualifiable performance.

Formative assessment can refer to any criteria to guide decisions about how best to continue learning. Public criteria can be used, along with self-referenced criteria, sometimes called ipsative criteria. These define achievement in a person on the basis of comparison with what has previously been accomplished. Progress may be massive or minute, or may not be possible. What 'progress' means depends on the individual's situation, needs, interests, talents and aspirations. This 4-year-old can suddenly read independently and reads a whole book. This 8-year-old is struggling to maintain eye contact as a means of communication. This 16-year-old has just given his first performance of a Chopin waltz. Here competition is within the individual. The focus is on maintaining quality of life and development.

> Because the focus is on learning, criteria used in formative assessment can include anything thought capable of affecting how the learners are and what they might do next. The quality of teaching, the use of resources and appropriateness of the environment, all can come under the scrutiny of assessors intent on removing blocks and boosting aids to learning. Here we see what formative assessment has in common with inclusive education.

A presumption made in and about summative assessment is that 'pure' learning can be elicited and graded. The examination is meant to be a window on what candidates are capable of. This may be why examinees forget the learning they produce for summative assessment. Having no authentic context for their performance, all but an aura of what it felt like is lost.

Summative assessment's validity and reliability stem from the standardization of context. The examinees face comparable, regulated tasks, and are meant to produce specified capabilities on demand, and at a supposedly representative and replicable level. Controlling the context gives summative assessment its high internal validity. But its external validity is correspondingly low: under more flexible conditions candidates might show more of what they are capable of, and more accurately.

One of the weaknesses and injustices of summative assessments is that learners may not be forewarned or prompted to show what they can do in terms of the criteria being used to judge them. Under formal conditions, and given sufficient personal and social awareness on the part of those being examined, summative assessment is experienced as *being assessed*: as surveillance. By contrast, learners are in a position to experience formative assessment as *doing something and learning*: as autonomous agents and partners in critical reflection. Performance is the object in summative assessment. What matters in formative assessment is the person.

Dylan Wiliam (1994) may have had this in mind when he recommended a move away from norm- and criterion-referenced assessment to 'construct-referenced' assessment, where 'the domain of assessment is holistic, rather than being defined in terms of precise objectives' (p. 59). He thought that

'What is required is a way of assessing authentic tasks on their own terms – in terms of what the student set out to do' (p. 54). Pessimistically, he doubted that 'any kind of explicit assessment scheme' could achieve that, though I suggest that principles of the kind given here could provide a basis for greater professional and public trust in formative processes and results.

Formative assessment tells teachers and learners about the learning, as it begins and while it is happening, so that learning may continue and be better for being assessed. Of course, if they have access to it, people other than teachers and learners might take note of formative assessment, but it is not addressed to third parties. It is concerned hardly at all with measurement, and with attainment as a sign of progress. It allows as many means of expression to learners, and as many indicators to assessors, in as many media, as are practicable.

> In formative assessment it does not matter that some facets of learners' capabilities are difficult to gauge. A distinctive feature of formative assessment is that the learning it reflects does not have to be wholly predicted. The unexpected can be taken into account. Formative assessment is valid insofar as it illuminates areas of learning that teachers and learners can use to inform further effort. It is reliable, not because the examined performance is decontextualized, but because it is rooted in a context that can be experienced for what it is. Given other engaging contexts and activities, a learner may be depended on to reproduce similar 'levels' of competence, or even show gains in their learning.

It is a strength of formative assessment that it can be used on occasions and under circumstances that allow learners to perform to their potential. It has high external validity. Its internal validity may be low because its contexts are not controlled other than to be safe and conducive to constructive and meaningful experience.

Summative assessment does not require learners to be interested in activity for its own sake. In fact, their success is probably better served by extrinsic or utilitarian interest. The learners' intrinsic interest in summatively assessed activity can detract from efforts to meet requirements. It is sensible to think of learning as suspended during summative assessment.

Extrinsic interest, aiming to be top for example, informs performance which is summatively assessed. And extrinsic interest, such as wanting to please the teacher, is not necessarily a barrier to learning which is formatively assessed. But for learning to come under learners' self-motivated adaptable control, what may start as extrinsic has to become intrinsic. Formative assessment promotes learners' interest in the quality of what they do for its own merit.

> Because learners are not expected through summative assessment to become autonomous, its provision does nothing to transform the learners' dependence or compliance. Because learners are expected through formative assessment to become autonomous, its provision is designed to enable learners to move from dependence on feedback to self advocacy as confident and competent monitors of their own activities.

It cannot be over-emphasized that formative assessment is concerned not with performance as such, but with learning. Mary Jane Drummond (1993: 13) defined assessment as 'The ways in which, in our everyday practice, we observe children's learning, strive to understand it, and then put our understanding to good use'. But that can hardly stand as a definition of summative assessment. The two systems differ in these respects:

Summative assessment has:	**Formative assessment has:**
no interest in what happens next, because the activity has no history and no future	'Now what?' as a key question, as well as 'Why do it?'
a focus on performance and attainment	a focus on learning and progress
a public audience	the individual learner and those who care for and teach her/him as audience
predictability and certainty as ideals	tolerance of unpredictability and ambiguity
controlled conditions	flexible conditions
high internal validity	low internal validity
low external validity	high external validity.

Learners need sufficient commitment to their activity to sustain their effort and its formative assessment. If the learners lose interest, they tend to abandon activity, forfeit formative assessment, and give into mere summative assessment. If they can be active in their assessment as well as truly engaged in their task, their interest is stimulated along with their learning.

Perspective and voice are fault lines between formative and summative modes of assessment. Formative assessment includes the learners' point of view. Summative assessment relies on appointed authorities' point of view.

The contrasts in learners' experience are clear:

	In formative assessment	**In summative assessment**
learners' intrinsic interest is:	desirable, even necessary	optional, perhaps an impediment
learners' active part in assessment is:	desirable, even necessary	denied, and impractical
criteria are:	self-made and/or taken from public sources, standards-oriented and/or person-centred, extensive, necessarily explicit, fluid, dynamic, formative	non-negotiable and taken from public sources, guarantees of standards, limited, implicit or explicit, stable, normative
learners' understanding of criteria is:	desirable, even necessary	advantageous, but not required
learners' goal of autonomy is:	implicit, if not explicit	irrelevant

Implications for policy

There seem to be lots of influences that prepare learners for summative assessment but comparatively few that prepare them for formative assessment. The first thing you can do is facilitate your pupils' interest in what they do as a basis for their developing interest in their learning. Chapter 2 outlined some strategies to that end. The second thing to do is to promote their critical reflection on what they do and what they learn. The 'Ten things to be clear about' in Chapter 3 offer a framework for this. The third thing to do is engage with public bodies and institutions to seek agreement about how purposes, processes and criteria are to be evaluated in education. The arguments made in this book are intended to inform debate and help improve what learners experience and achieve in school.

Some people seem to believe that education should promote values and practices that are characteristic of summative and at best transparent assessment: using prescription and one-way communication to create discriminatory, didactic classrooms, schools and forms of professional development. The majority of the voices in this book identify education's purposes and processes with values and practices that are characteristic of formative and interactive assessment: using dialogue and shared decision-making to create inclusive, participatory classrooms, schools and forms of institutional and professional development.

> The biggest obstacle to developing formative assessment may be the difficulty individuals and organizations have in extricating it and themselves from summative assessment. The dominance of high-status, high-stakes testing for the purpose of holding institutions to account does not help. Formative assessment's potential is to develop the part learners play in deciding purposes and criteria for their activities. This has a parallel, and possibly a root, in teachers' and assistants' capacity to co-determine with their leaders and managers the purposes and criteria for their professional and institutional development. This in turn is facilitated by government's enabling educational leaders and managers to co-determine the purposes and criteria for schools' provision of education.

Misguided efforts are sometimes made to 'improve' formative assessment by making it like summative assessment. But it does not serve learning to think public criteria matter most, to think test conditions have to apply, to think assessments should be documented with a public audience in mind. Formative assessment is ruined when it is made to fit in with summative assessment.

Throughout this book we have seen that the best premise for the development of formative assessment in lessons is collaborative action research, promoted and supported by confident, proactive leadership and management. This involves accepting the widest possible frame of reference for educational outcomes and increasing their public recognition.

Currently a very narrow set of indicators is highlighted. Of the five areas of achievement charted by Every Child Matters and Ofsted, official priority is consistently given to a single facet of attainment: the summative accounting of cohorts' academic performance at key transition points. This woefully neglects and scandalously undermines the other aims and results. These are:

- safety;
- health;
- enjoyment and achievement, which are registered less well by tests, better in qualitative records and celebrations of learning;
- contributions to the community;

- well-being shown in the capacity to sustain vital resources.

To our shame, we set out a full, valid, worthwhile agenda, and then pay insufficient attention to nine tenths of it.

The project behind this book presented evidence of how formative assessment informs and enhances learning across a complete spectrum of qualities and capabilities. The final chapter describes the project and gives it a research context. This should assist critical evaluation of the conclusion: that formative assessment has an essential role to play in the planning, conduct and assurance of an education system designed to promote autonomous citizenship.

16 The project's methodology and research context

This chapter describes the project that gave rise to this book, and locates it in the context of research. It answers the questions:

- How was the project designed and carried out?
- How do the project's conclusions fit with published research on formative assessment?

The Portsmouth Learning Community AfL project

The Portsmouth Learning Community was established in 2002 to raise standards of achievement, and ran for five years. It had three strands: colleagues learning from one another across institutional boundaries ('school-to-school learning'); pupils having a voice in educational decision-making ('student voice'); and assessment for learning (AfL, or formative assessment). This was not an experiment, but a mix of intervention, observation and collaboration between colleagues in the field and university team members.

For the AfL strand, at the invitation of leaders and teachers from 66 of the 72 schools and LA advisers, project team members ran and facilitated training sessions in schools and at inter-school meetings, met with working groups, visited and joined in lessons, and interviewed leaders, staff members and pupils. We liaised with LA personnel and steering groups, and commented on Keele surveys (1990) and schools' self evaluation forms. We reported progress, and made case studies and resources for teachers, pupils and leaders. Over the five years a budget of 380 person-days was spent on the University of Sussex AfL team. The LA also financed leaders' and staff members' release, as well as advisory and administrative support.

The role we negotiated was to assist and critique Portsmouth colleagues' planning, practice and self evaluation in AfL. We helped them link with one another and with people outside the city. Our promotion of school-to-school learning was informed by the national research project (Fielding et al., 2005), which concluded that 'joint practice development' was a better description and approach than 'transfer of good practice'. We followed that report's insight that professionals and organizations learn more effectively from one another when they build on existing relationships rather than have new ones imposed.

Colleagues became involved at different stages for different durations. They brought to the project different understandings about AfL and processes of development. Some were familiar with Shirley Clarke's conferences and books (e.g. 2001) and/or with the work of the King's College London University team (e.g. Black *et al.*, 2002). It was Shirley Clarke who provided an early round of training days for 14 primary schools, a role then taken over by the UoS team.

Colleagues had many distractions as reasons to defer working on AfL. Getting in the way for some were staff recruitment and retention, changes in personnel, structural reorganization and pressure of league table performance. Others thought such things as the government's Every Child Matters (2003) agenda encouraged AfL.

Some colleagues saw fragmentation and contradiction in what they felt was expected of them. Others were assertive and proactive in creating their own coherent agenda. An infant school headteacher spoke for the latter:

> *Possibly the biggest driver for development in the school has been giving the children the best we can, on all sorts of levels, not only in teaching and learning, but encouraging their overall development. Underpinning the children's learning is their well-being, their welfare. We started our children having a voice before it came onto the government's agenda. We know we are not there yet, but we are trying to make things coherent. There is a danger of operating things tangentially. We want pupil voice and assessment for learning all to become part of the school ethos. We have more embedding to do. We have had to be courageous to say no to some things. We are now tougher and more concentrated, and in control of how we develop. We have to have a deeply embedded philosophy to decide what we allow in and what we keep out. The mental health of the institution is dependent on people feeling that they can do what they do. Clearly we do what is statutory and then we look at other things, asking 'Does it fit?'*

Our intention was to contribute through AfL to 'an educational science in which each classroom is a laboratory, each teacher a member of the scientific community', as Lawrence Stenhouse (1976) saw it. So we tried to set an example of treating any home-grown, imported or imposed change to teaching and learning not as 'an unqualified recommendation but rather as a provisional specification claiming no more than to be worth putting to the test of practice' (Stenhouse, 1976). This, we knew, can cause or increase tensions, especially when statutory reform and public accountability dominate the scene.

We wanted to illuminate the spirit beyond the letter of AfL (see Marshall and Drummond, 2006). The letter is conveyed by techniques, such as making learning objectives and criteria visible, mind-mapping, modelling how to perform tasks, think-time, self and peer assessment, and traffic-lighting success against criteria (see Appendix 1). The spirit is conveyed by values and principles which underpin strategies. We tried to explain manifest differences in learners' lesson experiences and in teachers' experiences of professional and institutional development. We saw these differences as reflecting more than the choice of teaching or training technique. We thought differences were linked to alternative ethical dispositions and intentions.

We are indebted to others' research. Two sources were especially influential. The first was Harry Torrance's and John Pryor's 'convergence' and 'divergence' (1998): teaching and learning tend either to narrow down to fixed prescription, or to lead out to relative open-endedness and negotiated self-determination. The second was Paul Black's and colleagues' emphasis on learners grasping the purpose of their activity and taking decisions about it (2003).

Other writers further informed the approach we took. We built on research which proposes teaching is most effective when learners:

- are treated with patience, tolerance and reliability ('good enough care' as a condition for the development of a 'true self', D.W. Winnicott, 2006);
- are offered tasks which draw on and stretch what they can already do ('zone of proximal development', **ZPD**, Lev Vygotsky, 1978);
- work together and so deal with disagreement, which entails reconstructing their thinking ('the social roots of learning', Lev Vygotsky, 1978);
- are supported and challenged to solve problems ('scaffolding', Jerome Bruner, 1983);
- control what they can control, in order to pursue their own goals ('self-efficacy', Albert Bandura, 1997);
- see the 'big picture' and pay timely attention to details and sub-skills ('focal' and 'tacit' learning, Michael Polanyi, 1962);
- receive affirmative feedback, enabling them to learn from setbacks as well as triumphs ('self-theories' and 'mindsets', Carol Dweck, 2000);
- look at what goes well and build on that, rather than concentrating on what doesn't go well ('solution-focused practice', Steve de Shazer, 2005);
- know what to do when they don't know what to do ('learning to learn', Guy Claxton, 2005);

- are listened to ('student voice', Jean Rudduck, e.g. in John MacBeath et al., 2003);
- investigate many aspects of school life and have their findings taken seriously ('students as researchers', Michael Fielding and Sara Bragg, 2003).

Most colleagues welcomed the challenges of reflecting on their practice and being offered our outsider's view. Uncertainty and unpredictability emerged as hallmarks of enjoyable and effective learning and development in the accounts colleagues gave.

Those who were less inclined to experiment and share ideas had many reasons: the pupils made it difficult; they felt they were doing well enough; senior leaders gave no backing; there was too much content to cover and no time for extras; too much pressure to improve test results.

We offered colleagues in the field this initial definition:

> Assessment for Learning involves *communication* and *dialogue* between students and teachers. It means that teachers and students *reflect* on and *evaluate* their work. It helps students to develop greater self-awareness, self-confidence and independence, leading to greater *autonomy* in their learning. Implementing AfL means *developing processes* in the classroom, in teams and departments, at a whole-school level and beyond.
>
> (Blanchard *et al.*, 2004a: 1)

As the project unfolded, we developed a model and vocabulary of 'transparency', 'interactivity' and 'critical awareness' (see Chapters 1 and 3), terms which entered the language of many colleagues we worked with. We did not offer prescription.

We and, less often, colleagues in the field made notes of every encounter and event. To these sometimes were added collective statements made in workshop and plenary sessions, as well as audio and video recordings. Those involved amended and approved the records as valid and acceptable. We saw these data as belonging to participating colleagues, and guarded against reporting over their heads or behind their backs.

Our reporting was designed to inform critical reflection and experiment. It culminated in the production of a practical guide (Johns and Blanchard, 2007), based on the framework of 'Ten things to be clear about'. (The model and framework are explained in Chapter 3, and shown in Appendix 2.)

The comments below cover the range. There is admittedly a bias towards positive examples and quotations. We worked more with colleagues who saw the project's potential:

Junior school teacher: *The session did not give us the answers we were looking for. It didn't take our school forward. We have heard these ideas before.*

Primary school teachers: *Initially I thought that this was going to be a checking up procedure and had reservations about the interview. However, the opportunity for discussion has been reassuring in that I feel I'm doing the right sort of thing. I thought that the compilation report [Blanchard et al., 2004a] was good.*

This project has given me new things to think about that I hadn't thought about before. It has highlighted things that I didn't think were a problem.

It has helped to develop me further as a reflective practitioner.

Infant school headteacher: *I think it's been good to have other people who've had an overview across the city who've been able to alert people to different things that are happening outside the school and outside the School Improvement Service or Learning and Achievement. Because they [LA personnel] do fulfil that to a certain extent, but there's a kind of slightly mixed role there because obviously they are part of your employer. Whereas Sussex University, alright they have a contract with them, but it is a step further away. That's not to be critical, but it's a different role, with the changes they have had. It's a critical friend role, I think. Local authority inspectors do fulfil that role but they're in a more difficult position because they are also accountable. They have a more ambiguous role.*

Secondary school teacher: *I think the success is because of my involvement with the Sussex team ... For something to be wise rather than just an idea, you need to know that you know. ... There's a world of difference between agreeing with an idea to feeling that you've experienced something, changed your practice because of it, and are now an advocate of that idea.*

Primary school teachers: *The children are more involved in their own and each other's learning.*

Children are more forward in raising concerns about their work, and talking about their learning.

There has been most change with SEN children. They have become more open and enjoy being able to refer visually to class targets and their own targets.

Infant school teacher: *I see AfL as taking teaching back to what it should be, away from the pressure to produce evidence all the time. It is about the quality of pupils' work and learning, whereby they demonstrate their growing maturity, rather than getting right or wrong answers.*

Junior school teacher: *I like to reach out and touch and inspire the children. There are some still at a distance, and I know that if they wanted to they could achieve great things. I am really pleased with the impact of what I have been trying. Sometimes it's quite overwhelming to see how well it is going. I will definitely use these methods with other classes I teach in the future. I am comfortable with my teaching style.*

We did not treat our data to any quantitative or statistical analysis, except in respect of the Keele Survey (Keele University, 1990). We kept feeding back what we found in much the same way as this book presents argument, narrative and illustration, so that themes and patterns in colleagues' and pupils' experiences might be teased out and learned from. (An overview of our findings is given in Chapter 1.)

The final report of the Portsmouth Learning Community (Fielding et al., 2008: 20) concluded:

> The data suggest that across the LA standards have risen over the five-year period and that in some schools where standards rose, the staff attribute this wholly or partly to developments arising from the Portsmouth Learning Community.

What follows is an attempt to place the project in a context of research relating to formative assessment.

A research context

We were aware of an extensive literature on 'school effectiveness' and 'school improvement'. Our approach was pragmatic and resonates with Alma Harris's (2002) stimulating overview.

We were prepared for our project to be part of a wide-ranging and ongoing undertaking in a climate of high-stakes accountability which militates against trust, long-term thinking and risk-taking (see Reay and Wiliam, 1999). We took Black's and Wiliam's (1998) caution seriously that 'the changes in classroom practice that are needed are central rather than marginal, and have to be incorporated by each teacher into his or her practice' (p. 62).

We suggest that our model of 'transparency' and 'interactivity' and framework of 'Ten things to be clear about' might revise the King's College four-part construction of formative assessment, as mentioned by Marshall and Drummond (2006: 147):

> [It] appears that the four original headings, under which AfL practice was conceived—questioning, feedback, sharing criteria and self assessment—need revision. What we have called the spirit of AfL is instantiated in the

way teachers conceptualize and sequence the tasks undertaken by pupils in the lesson.

We believe we have defined distinct elements in the conceptualizing and sequencing of tasks. We propose that the quality of resulting performance depends on the extent to which teachers enable their pupils to take responsibility for decisions that affect their activity. This accords with Fielding's student voice typology: transparency mapping approximately onto 'stages' 1 and 2, interactivity onto 'stages' 3 and 4:

Transparency

1. Students as data source: receiving a better informed pedagogy
2. Students as active respondents: discussing current approaches to teaching and learning

Interactivity

3. Students as co-enquirers: working with adults to ask and answer questions about how lessons and schooling work
4. Students as knowledge creators: planning, researching, interpreting, reporting findings

(adapted from Fielding, 2004)

Relating this specifically to lessons, we agree with Sadler's characterization (1989: 122–3) of the empowerment and metacognition that are entailed in formative assessment:

[S]tudents have to be able to judge the quality of what they are producing and be able to regulate what they are doing during the doing of it. ... Formative assessment includes both feedback and self-monitoring. The goal of many instructional systems is to facilitate the transition from feedback to self-monitoring.

We associate the transition from transparency to interactivity with a progression from feedback provided by teachers and assistants to self monitoring by learners. On this view, classroom learning depends on learners having some understanding of how and why tasks are designed and ordered as they are. We saw many of our teachers promoting this by means of mind-mapping or shared topic preparation, some also managing to make the traditional gambit of question-and-answer serve this purpose.

> There is a sense in which classroom learning can be made to approximate to naturalistic learning by forms of pedagogy which support self governance. We suggest that effective education is based on transparency, mediated by interactivity, and fulfilled in autonomous projects. Our framework of critical awareness cannot prescribe teaching, but can inform attitudes and behaviours that are conducive to the development of learners' participation, motivation and autonomy.

Our findings reflect Flanagan's (2004) review of research in psychology relating to early child development, and extend her commentary to learning throughout the years of schooling. Her identification of receptiveness and responsiveness as crucial features of effective pedagogy points to the functions we found in formative assessment and interactive teaching and learning:

> [The] more sensitive an adult is to a child's competence and the more the adult exposes the child to processes necessary for problems-solving, the more the child should improve.
>
> (Flanagan, 2004: 73)

In our view, the processes necessary for problem solving are prepared by decision-making about important aspects of activity. Our evidence adumbrates Flanagan's portrayal of teaching as fostering interest, illuminating key performative components, being accessible yet challenging, facilitating rather than dictating, and sponsoring autonomy:

> The tutor has the task of engaging and maintaining children's interest, simplifying the task so as to reduce the number of steps required to reach the target, highlighting those that are relevant, and providing demonstrations for children to imitate. Such a technique demands special skills of the tutor, chiefly to ensure that the demands they make are within the children's ZPD, but also that they guide children rather than telling them what to do ... Children must organize new information for themselves by integrating it into existing hierarchies or adapting hierarchies to fit new situations.
>
> (Flanagan, 2004: 75)

Our framework's elements bring coherence to this construction of teaching, where 'questioning', 'feedback', 'sharing criteria' and 'self assessment' offer disparate concepts. Those four headings imply teachers' agency, except when learners self assess. Our ten things refer to how teachers *and* learners implicitly and explicitly set up, revise, judge and extend their activities, and thereby learn. Their significance is indicated by a special school deputy headteacher:

School assessment is at best something which is part of a continuous process, enabling the student to make choices about activities and experiences, supported by the staff's gathering of information about the student's efforts, sifting and drawing conclusions about how best to celebrate and build on progress. Key forms of assessment are observation and dialogue, and one of the most important means for staff to share perceptions is their daily team review meetings every afternoon when they ask: 'What went well? How could things be improved? Where next? Specific concerns?'

That compressed statement illustrates two fundamental aspects of improvements to teaching and learning identified by Black et al. (2006): that learners should make choices, which signifies the intention to promote their autonomy; and that, in their professional and curriculum development, teachers should learn, much as pupils do, which signifies congruity of means and ends:

[A] common characteristic of practices that improve learning is summed up by the term 'learning autonomy' ... [such] that the learner can not only give meaning to the learning, but that she can also create new learning tools. (p. 129)

Insofar as teachers are also learners, and their schools can be described as learning organizations, we believe that these insights may be equally applicable to learning at these levels also. (p. 130)

Creating new learning tools entails teachers responding to learners' dynamic uniqueness and being prepared to hold them through the consequences of their choices. An infant school teacher put it like this:

I believe in not sticking rigidly to rules. There's no one individual model of a normal child. All have different needs. To meet those needs you have to be flexible. . . Helping them cooperate and be independent is stuff I'm doing all the time.

We propose that it is through clarifying decisive factors in activity that pupils in a classroom, as well as professionals in an organization, give their learning meaning, create new learning tools and experience autonomy. In our view it is through awareness of critical elements in activities that learners manage, as Sadler (1989) saw it, 'to develop *their* evaluative knowledge, thereby bringing them within the guild of people who are able to determine quality using multiple criteria' (p. 135).

Dialogue is the medium: dialogue about activity that has yet to start, that is ongoing, and that has been brought to a close. We came to see

the social, cognitive and affective acts of determining ethos, establishing prior knowledge, setting objectives, and so on, as the means by which learners and teachers realize their capacity to learn.

We believe we have what Black et al. (2006) fell short of developing as a rationale for the generation of effective learning in lessons:

[O]ur experience ... shows that teachers find [AfL practices] effective across a range of school subjects, and in primary and in secondary subject contexts, but that they need some adaptation for optimum effect in each. A rationale for reconciling these generic and subject specific features has yet to be developed.

(Black et al., 2006: 131)

We suggest that our framework of critical awareness, explored in detail in Chapter 4 to 13, constitutes a rationale, and that adaptations for different subjects, though potentially useful, are not intrinsically necessary. We concur with Black (2005: 133) that:

[It] is striking that the alignment of several aspects of classroom practice within the formative focus has led many of the teachers involved to rethink their roles as teachers. This is a radical effect with implications at many levels, so any exploration has to look both at a micro level, into the nature of this change, and at a macro level, into the contexts and conditions in which it is being developed.

Contexts and conditions, which support formative assessment, allow teachers and learners to bring from tacit to focal awareness, hence under control, facets of performance that generate the intended capability. This is what Polanyi (1962) called 'connoisseurship'.

There is more to this than practitioners', or even leaders' and managers', volition and expertise. There are objective conditions, brought about by vision, policy, strategy and funding, which are more or less conducive to the quality and scope of the development at stake here.

The change consists in teachers being transparent about the determinants of quality in activity, hence the ingredients of learning, and in learners' interactive and ultimately autonomous engagement with the same. The development requires time, resource and status being given to learning about learning through collaborative action research.

Facilitating or inhibiting this are priorities set by government and educational administration. If these are unsympathetic toward autonomy as a goal, efforts to implement just some of its superficial benefits fail. If, in their provisions, government and administration signal their approval of formative assessment's tenets and processes, the resulting congruity and synergy inform and sustain development. The Every Child Matters and Ofsted inspection framework promotes formative, inclusive principles and practices, but, when it comes to evaluation and accountability, this is contradicted by headlining of narrowly conceived academic results.

Our evidence indicates more than that there *may* be a parallel between pupils' learning and professionals' development. We believe our project shows that formative assessment achieves its authentic benefits when there is congruity between teaching in lessons and the leadership of whole-school improvement. And this depends on the wider political climate. An infant school headteacher pinpointed the integrity of micro and macro levels:

> *An important thing about this school is that the adults here see themselves as learners, wanting to improve themselves. We develop adults here as much as the children.*

> When teachers, teaching assistants, leaders and managers experience in professional and whole-school development the very processes that they want pupils to experience in lessons, they are enabled to understand formative assessment in lived practice. This is process knowledge, which imbues the communication of subject knowledge.

Our framework's ten elements should not be summatively assessed, even if valid, reliable measures could be found. We take Sadler's view (2002: 50–1), seeing clarity about those elements as the means by which learners act on forces and factors that drive what they do and learn:

> Learning in a goal-directed way typically draws simultaneously on a large number of variables: knowledge, skills, attitudes, aptitudes, goal clarity, problem structuredness, contextual conditions, solution constraints, expected rewards, consequences of alternative outcomes and, of course, dispositions to tackle the learning task... Anything that makes it easier to lose sight of the big picture is potentially risky, including research or practice that focuses too intensively on a small subset of the variables. Explicit measurement of some of them would inevitably intensify such a focus. (pp 50–1)

Using any of the ten elements prescriptively would not be helpful. Capable performance, hence learning, depends on subjectively meaningful activity, commitment and flow, subtly informed by reflection. We believe our project has produced evidence that teachers' and learners' critical and heightened awareness helps them be deliberate about what they do and what they learn, without intensifying self-consciousness to the point of distortion or inhibition.

The ten elements – ethos, prior knowledge, intention, interest, criteria, method, resilience, achievement, improvement and application – provide an analytic, dynamic, holistic frame for teachers' and learners' attention and autonomy. This could also be said to apply to government and administration. We may ask whether policy- and strategy-makers can be as adept in formative and responsive practice as the best teachers and leaders whose work in schools they affect.

Appendix 1
Assessment for learning: Reviewing current practice

In your lessons do these things happen:

regularly [two ticks]   occasionally [one tick]   never [no tick] ?

Underline what is most important.

- planning for *learning* rather than merely *doing*
- deciding how to work together and how to organize the classroom/space/resources (groundrules and ethos)
- reviewing what we already know (recapping), and deciding what we might want to learn (mind-mapping)
- making objectives visible, and referring to them
- clarifying what the pupils *must*, *should* and *could* try to achieve (differentiation)
- having individual and/or group targets
- seeing how this topic links with others (the 'big picture')
- exploring why this might be important to learn (the rationale)
- defining what counts as good (criteria)
- making criteria visible, and referring to them
- knowing what steps to take (having a clear method)
- having models to work from
- using talk partners and helping one another
- everyone having time to think about answers to questions
- asking fewer yes/no questions, more open questions
- seeing how difficulties and mistakes can help learning (developing resilience and perseverance)
- discussing what helps and what hinders learning
- having positive feedback referring to objectives and criteria
- self assessment and peer assessment (e.g. using markschemes)
- highlighting successes and strengths
- having time and guidance to improve performance and develop learning (doing corrections, revisions and extension work)
- taking a teaching role
- discussing how learning can be applied in other contexts.

Reflection A1.1

These are regular and confident features of my/our AfL practice:

· ·

· ·

· ·

I/We can explores these features further by:

· ·

· ·

· ·

Analysing and building on what works: a strategy for collaboration and development

- Talk about AfL strategies with colleagues.
- Explain AfL strategies currently being used (e.g. using the format above), so that colleagues can learn from each other.
- Discuss how AfL can be developed.
- Arrange for coaching if it is wanted.
- Identify AfL strategies to be developed (e.g. using the format above), and keep these as a record and resource.
- Develop ways of collecting and communicating AfL strategies across the school (e.g. using the format below). Refer to these in team plans and reviews, performance management records, the SEF ... alongside displays and records of pupils' work, portfolios of moderated work (see Appendix 5) ...

Examine specific AfL strategies (e.g. from the list on page 159), and share these in your team or across the school. These can be in current use, or in the planning stage.

AfL strategy: . . . .

What our pupils need to know and be able to do to engage with this:

. . . .

. . . .

How we explain it to our pupils:

. . . .

. . . .

How it helps their learning:

. . . .

. . . .

Watch out for:

. . . .

. . . .

Analysing one strategy: an example

AfL strategy: Pupils help decide criteria.

What our pupils need to know and be able to do to engage with this:

They need to think about the topic or activity. It helps if they make a connection with something they are interested in or familiar with, or can imagine. It helps if they are used to the idea of having criteria to guide them, but this is not essential.

How we explain it to our pupils:

E.g. *For this task I am giving you one criterion, and I want you to decide on some more, according to what you think is important.*

You have to write in sentences that start with a capital letter. What else do you think you can try to do to make your writing top quality?

We will use the criterion I suggest and the criteria you suggest, to see what is successful in your work, and what can be improved.

How it helps their learning:

They feel more committed to what they are doing, if they have helped decide what counts as good.
Owning their criteria helps learners at the start and when they meet problems. It helps them assess themselves and one another.
It gives depth to their learning. They are not just doing as they are told. They internalize the key issue of what quality is.
They are learning how to learn, especially when they discuss the part that deciding criteria plays in what they do.

Watch out for:

- How the criteria serve the overall objectives for the lesson or topic.
- There is no right number of criteria. Sometimes pupils can handle five to ten. Sometimes they need to have just one or two to concentrate on.
- Be open about the fact that there has to be more to the task than the things listed as criteria: the stated criteria are to help focus on useful and important aspects of the task.
- Criteria are not a recipe: talking about how to judge quality is not the same as deciding how to carry out a task. Method gets the job done; criteria focus on quality and raise standards.
- Be prepared to trust your pupils. They can learn from things that don't turn out as planned, as well as from things that turn out well.
- See their confidence grow as they take on the role of expert and test their ideas against the evidence of outcomes.

Appendix 2
Ten things to be clear about: checklist and observation format

Tick what you regularly do. Underline what is most important.

Circle where pupils help make decisions.

[1] How do we work together?
e.g. groundrules; think-time; learning partners; deciding and choosing; helping one another; being treated as an individual; being open about not knowing
[2] What do we know about this topic?
e.g. recapping; mind-mapping; learning walls
[3] What are we trying to achieve?
e.g. focus on learning; key questions; big picture; targets; displays
[4] What might be interesting about this?
e.g. fun; play; relevance; challenge; purpose
[5] How can we know how well we do?
e.g. criteria for assessment/quality/success
[6] How do we tackle it?
e.g. modelling; checklist; roles; timings
[7] What can we do when we get stuck or go wrong?
e.g. routines; posters; learning partners; talking about how mistakes can help; talking about what 'ability' is
[8] What have we achieved?
e.g. products, presentations and exhibitions; self-checking; feedback; using criteria to highlight strengths; traffic lighting
[9] How can we improve?
e.g. self-checking; comment marking; giving time for improvement; extending
[10] How can we use what we learn?
e.g. transferring skills and knowledge across subjects; relevance to life; teaching someone else

---

Reflection A2.1

This is a strength:

. . . .

. . . .

. . . .

An area for development is in my/our formative assessment:

. . . .

. . . .

. . . .

Ten things to be clear about: observation format

What we say and do | *What they say and do*

1. How do we work together?

2. What do we know about this?

3. What are we trying to achieve?

4. What might be interesting about this?

5. How can we know how well we're doing?

6. How are we going to tackle it?

7. What can we do when we get stuck or go wrong?

8. What have we achieved?

9. How can we improve?

10. How can we use what we learn?

Note to visitors about making judgements

This statement advises caution when evaluating activities in complex settings. It comes from a secondary pupil referral unit lead teacher, and was made as part of a policy review. Advisers and inspectors are asked to take account of developments teachers and assistants are engaged in, and to probe the decisions they make:

> It is important for those who hold staff to account to appreciate that the staff's professional decision-making aims to strike the most productive balance possible between teaching and learning. Staff have to learn to challenge students without alienating them. This is a very dynamic process. Staff use their knowledge of the students and their ever-changing moods and responses to create the best possible context for security, progress and achievement. This can involve introducing more play-oriented activity and the apparent suspension of overtly academic work. The flexible disapplication of national curriculum or timetabled activities is one formal aspect of this, but so too is the informal, minute-to-minute and session-by-session adaptation by staff to the students' present behaviours and attitudes.
>
> Documentation and statistical data, although conscientiously maintained in several different forms, do little justice to staff's complex and shifting analysis and decision-making. Visitors to the centre are invited, before and after observed sessions, to explore with members of staff how they construct their expectations, plans, assessments and evaluations in any specific instance and generally. When visitors can discuss with staff how they see things, better understanding is developed about the quality of provision and outcomes.

Reflection A2.2

We have this protocol and approach to lesson observation:

. . . .

. . . .

. . . .

We can improve our arrangements for lesson observations by:

. . . .

. . . .

. . . .

Appendix 3
Format for planning small-scale development

Name/Team: . . . .   Date: . . . .

Aims

Benefits

Evidence

Evaluation activities

Next steps

Appendix 4
Feedback and marking policy

Delete, amend, and add items to reflect your practice.

- Marking can mean responding to pupils' work, whether in conversation or through writing: spoken as well as written feedback.
- Pupils know the purpose of individual pieces of work.
- Pupils can say what the unit of work as a whole is about and can see what part individual pieces of work have in 'the bigger picture'.
- Pupils understand how their work is to be assessed: criteria are explicit.
- Pupils use markschemes and apply criteria themselves: they assess their own and one another's work.
- Pupils know when they can expect their work to be commented on and returned.
- Pupils understand the meaning and purpose of any score, grade, or level used.
- Comments are linked to lesson objectives and individual pupils' targets.
- Comments focus on criteria, are positive in overall tone, and are personalized, e.g. using the pupil's name.
- More often than not, the pupils are given time to do something with the marking they receive.
- Pupils know what the follow-up is to any piece of work: e.g. finishing off, practising certain skills, developing the work in certain ways, doing corrections.
- Teachers sometimes correct single errors, but they routinely look for opportunities to teach patterns, key skills and concepts. They do this through having the pupils do follow-up work. E.g. the pupils use special notebooks or pages in their exercise books to collect word families or concepts, information-webs, etc.
- Correction or proof-reading looks like this:

> in the margin	means	*Look along this line to find an error to put right*
underlining	means	*Here is the error*
correction in the margin	means	*I have put the error right for you to learn from*

The following are examples of colleagues' reviewing their practice.

This statement was made by a teacher and teacher-trainee following some lesson observations and discussions about principles for marking. They agreed that feedback should:

- *be close to the performance, on the spot, and help correct misunderstandings or skill deficits;*
- *inform dialogue;*
- *prompt/guide students' follow-up or next activity;*
- *dovetail with points in a lesson, e.g. final plenary review;*
- *look forward as well as back;*
- *refer to explicit, clear criteria;*
- *assist self and/or peer assessment;*
- *be varied, sometimes low key, sometimes intensive, often spoken, sometimes written;*
- *refer to the purpose of the activity.*

And this statement was made by the staff of a junior school during an INSET day, as a way of revising their policy:

Our understanding of Assessment for Learning

- *Assessments are made by teachers and support staff who actively involve the pupils, particularly through talk.*
- *We help the pupils to see where they are now, and what to do next.*
- *We help the pupils to be aware of their learning and think honestly about their progress.*
- *We use assessments to inform planning.*
- *There is a continuous, ongoing, developmental, reflective cycle of planning, doing and reviewing.*
- *This informs short and long term progression.*
- *Goals are realistic, achievable and relevant to the pupils' learning needs.*
- *AfL helps scaffold the pupils' activities.*
- *It helps the pupils make cognitive links, e.g. through mind-mapping.*
- *It helps the pupils gain immediate satisfaction that they have succeeded, and this supports their long term progression.*
- *It is constructivist.*
- *It builds on what the pupils already know and can do.*
- *It is evaluative.*
- *It is individualized and supports differentiation in the setting of tasks.*
- *It helps us improve our strategies.*
- *AfL shows which pupils have understood and achieved tasks.*
- *It can include the parents.*

Key elements in our marking

Given that everything cannot be legislated for and flexibility is needed:

- *We encourage the pupils to see the purpose of the work.*
- *Pupils write their learning objectives in their books, and are helped when necessary.*
- *The criteria are made clear whenever possible.*
- *Sometimes pupils use the criteria to mark one another's work.*
- *Staff use criteria to focus marking, and this may mean response is brief.*
- *Feedback is spoken more often than written.*
- *We help the pupils to interpret their feedback.*
- *Comments sometimes prompt the pupils to do something so time is given to allow them to do the follow-up.*

Reflection A4.1

Feedback helps our pupils to make progress by:

. . . .

. . . .

. . . .

Our pupils assess their own, and one another's, progress and achievement in these ways:

. . . .

. . . .

. . . .

We can improve these practices by:

. . . .

. . . .

. . . .

Appendix 5
Keeping examples of pupils' work and running moderation meetings

Suggested stages of a moderation meeting

1. A teacher shows (or, if there is no writing or product or recording, talks about) an example of a pupil's work, and explains its background.
2. Group members put questions to the presenting teacher for clarification.
3. Colleagues discuss the pupil's achievement, using their own notions of progress and achievement as well as level or grade criteria, without assigning a final level or grade.
4. Colleagues seek consensus on a level/grade, and the presenting teacher compares her/his own provisional judgement with what colleagues propose.
5. The group explores next steps in learning.
6. The group summarizes what they have been learning about:
   - how they teach X;
   - how pupils learn;
   - how they assess and record progress;
   - what the team/school does well and how it might develop further.

A primary school's statement about moderation

What we value in our moderation of pupils' work: points towards policy made during INSET on AfL

- *We have time to study or learn about the piece of work we are going to discuss.*
- *We focus on what makes it level n, and why it isn't level n+1 or level n−1.*
- *We refer to specific criteria, e.g. professionally or commercially produced schemes, and where there are conflicting criteria we explore those.*

- *We ask questions for clarification.*
- *We clarify points relating to the criteria and weightings, e.g. whether this is an assessment 'of best fit' or whether there is a number of instances that has to be shown.*
- *We clarify requirements relating to conditions/independence in the children's performance.*
- *We give a human appreciative response as well as technically analysing features of performance.*
- *We seek consensus.*
- *We consider how the learning can be taken forward.*
- *We keep some samples of moderated work in a portfolio as a way of showing our approach to standardization and some of its results.*

Reflection A5.1

How often do we have moderation meetings?

. . . .

Our key objectives for these meetings are:

. . . .

. . . .

. . . .

We can give these meetings the best chance of success by:

. . . .

. . . .

. . . .

Appendix 6
Surveying pupils' perceptions using ten key statements

- Tell your pupils to give honest answers so as to help you do the best for them.
- Do examples with the pupils to help them understand the statements and how to respond. Emphasize they decide.
- Talk with your pupils about what the time words mean, e.g. 'often' = more than once a week or in most lessons, 'rarely' = maybe once in a term, etc.
- Tell your pupils how you will use the results, and discuss how they can play a part in developing how lessons are run.

Please, write what you think is true for you in lessons:

3 for *often*, 2 for *sometimes*, 1 for *rarely*, 0 for *never*.

1. We talk with our teacher/s about how we are going to work together, e.g. agreeing groundrules and other helpful things. ☐

2. When I start an activity in class, I think about what I already know, understand, and can do. ☐

3. I think about what I am going to learn. ☐

4. When I am working in class, I think about what my interest is. ☐

5. I know how my teacher and I are going to judge my success. ☐

6. When I start an activity in class, I think about how I am going to do it. ☐

7. I think about how I can deal with difficulties and keep going. ☐

8. When I finish, I see what I have done well. ☐

9. I find out how I can improve what I do. ☐

10. I find out how I can apply what I learn in the future. ☐

You can build up a picture of how pupils feel about their experiences in lessons.

Here is a summary of key points that came out of a survey of pupils' views in one school. How typical do you think these perceptions are? Would your pupils agree?

How do we want to be treated?

> *Treat me as an individual.*
> *Don't make me feel ashamed.*
> *Be fair, be consistent.*
> *Listen to me.*

How do we like to do things?

> *Know what you're doing.*
> *Do something about the troublemakers.*
> *Let us have purpose and variety in our activities.*
> *Let us get on with it, and actually do something.*
> *Let us choose.*
> *Let us work together.*
> *Get everyone involved. And make it fun – at least sometimes.*
> *Let us do things that stretch us sometimes.*

What feedback do we need? What makes us want to learn?

> *Stickers, sanctions, satisfaction, specifics.*
> *Talk to me.*
> *Help me improve.*

Reflection A6.1

We can learn more about our pupils' perceptions by:

. . . .

. . . .

. . . .

Appendix 7
Six lessons observed

Year R Dance

These notes on a reception class's dance lesson show how the framework of 'Ten things to be clear about' (see Appendix 2) can be used to chart significant features in teaching and learning.

Teacher's words and actions	Pupils' words and actions
[1] Being clear about how they work together	
T models and joins in with activity. E.g. *I've got to remember – I get so excited I forget.* Getting changed into PE kit, going to the hall, having sound-system, knowing they are working towards a possible display of their dance: all of these signal an active, practical, joint, communicative activity and ethos. The T's tone and behaviour convey 'This is fun; we can do this; we can get better at it; let's have a go and learn together as we go'.	Ps engage in the activities of dance and group discussion and reflection: their behaviour demonstrates their understanding of and enthusiasm for a social, kinaesthetic experience.
[2] Being clear about what they already know/understand/ can do	
T questions the Ps about their previous lesson: *Can you remember, what were your three animals? What's the first thing we need to do?*	Ps say what their chosen animals were/are. Ps chorus: *Warm up.*

*We warm up so we don't hurt
our bodies when stretching.*
T asks the Ps to explain the
key criteria for their dance.

Ps respond accurately: *Levels, speeds,
shapes, pathways.*

[3] Being clear about what they are going to try to learn, and why

Key elements displayed ready
on the flipchart.
T refers occasionally to the
physical health dimension to
dance: *Feel your hearts, breathing . . .*

Pupils use cards for the key criteria.
See above, [2].

[4] Being clear about their interest in the topic/activities

T engages the pupils in the story
of the Lion King.

Pupils make decisions and choices
according to their interests and
preferences. E.g. *Can I be a hare?*

[5] Being clear about how they can judge success

Success criteria are displayed on
the flipchart and referred to
fluently and constructively
throughout the lesson. E.g.
Show off strong shapes.

Ps repeat and refer to their success
criteria in how they develop their
dance and explicitly when asked.

[6] Being clear about how to tackle the activities

During the warm-up: *Remember
your space bubble.*
Then, *Get your start positions.*
T cues the pupils by referring to
the success criteria. There is a
rhythm of practise–show–talk–
consider–improve.
There are reminders, e.g.
Dancing is a quiet thing, OK?
During activities T prompts,
e.g. *Can you feel . . .?*

The Ps' involvement, energy,
cooperation, and commitment
show their willingness to tackle the
activities in the spirit intended.

[7] Being clear about how to persevere and deal with difficulty

As one boy finds it difficult

Ps adapt their performance in the

to contain his energy (and desire to be different and have attention for himself?), T guides and models for him how to join in appropriately. Consistent reference to the success criteria scaffolds progressive development in performance.

light of comments and advice from the T and one another.

[8] Being clear about what they do well

T explains the TA *Will take photos today showing the best positions.*
T frequently indicates how performance matches the success criteria: *Good by Joseph, changing direction. Good space finding, people. Fantastic!*
T praises Ps for their peer and self evaluations.

The class divided into two, makes peer observation, taking one success criterion per two or three Ps.
Ps use thumbs up/down to show satisfaction with their performance.

[9] Being clear about how to improve

T refers to success criteria throughout.
When I was watching, I saw a few bits to make better. Can I tell you what I think? Some people forget and sprint. Remember to look like an animal. I saw some people getting better, but we're still on a roundabout (i.e. not varying direction).

So too do the Ps.
Ps individually diagnose aspects of their dance they want to improve: E.g. *Checking my pathways. Speed. Direction . . .*
Ps respond to question about how to develop further: *Do it again. We're on a roundabout.*

Year 3 Numeracy

The notes on this lesson, and on the following Year 6 literacy lesson, are taken from records written by consultant Ken Hann. The approach he used was loosely based on a coaching model. He and the teacher always agreed a focus which highlighted one or more of the AfL strategies colleagues were developing. It was not an inspection, and there was no threat. The records he made were initially for the teachers' eyes only, and then, after discussion and confirmation from them, reports were logged for the project as a whole.

The lesson

The lesson began with an oral/mental session using known facts to solve a puzzle. The pupils used talking partners to discuss answers and then communicate with the teacher. They were encouraged not to put hands up as pupils would be chosen to answer. The lesson then moved into its main focus with a displayed learning objective: *Can I multiply using the grid method?* The pupils used whiteboards to do a simple sum by way of the array method, and then looked at a more complicated example where a different method might make the calculation easier. The grid method was discussed. After working though some examples using talking partners and the whiteboards, the class moved into groups for guided and independent work.

During the plenary the pupils completed a grid on the **IWB** and discussed whether they had been successful using the hands up/out straight/down method.

Commentary

The pupils are enthusiastic and willing to put effort into all the tasks asked of them. The atmosphere in the classroom is delightful, being both purposeful and supportive.

They are comfortable using learning objectives and discussed suitable success criteria readily. Good progress has been made here in breaking down the more general success criteria in the planning into more understandable steps which show a route to success.

When asked to 'traffic light' their work they did this readily. The use of shutting eyes and then showing by hand signals whether they had understood the task works well. The pupils feel comfortable to show that they need more help without everyone being able to see.

The 'wait time' and talking partners works well, the pupils readily turning to the person next to them. They stayed on task most of the time.

Although encouraged not to put their hands up, this is obviously an almost automatic response. They were not thrown by someone else being asked. In time this response should lessen, if they are regularly reminded and there is seen to be no advantage in it.

They are open about their work and discuss and share readily with partners or in groups.

Suggestions for extending good practice

Continuing to develop the use of success criteria through example and discussion with them in all subjects will involve the pupils even more in their learning. They are already showing a readiness to be engaged.

Persevere with 'no hands up', as this does help to engage everyone and open up discussion.

I think the class would be able to become involved in a more extended form of questioning, although it may be easier to begin this in subjects other than maths.

Instead of asking a closed question, you could: give a range of answers for them to choose from; turn the question into a statement and ask them to consider its value; make a statement that is obviously wrong and ask them to consider it; give the answer and ask for the question; take an opposing view point, etc.

Year 6 Literacy

The lesson

A painting was used to stimulate discussion. The learning objective was displayed and discussed. In groups they discussed what the person in the painting was thinking about, and they offered their ideas to the class. A second picture was displayed and a similar exercise undertaken. This time the pupils discussed in pairs and then wrote a few sentences.

At this point the class was asked to offer suitable success criteria so that they could measure how well they were doing.

Four pictures in total were displayed and a choice made as to which one to use. A paragraph was then written about what the subject was thinking.

During the plenary a selection was read out and checked against the success criteria. Most pupils were happy to read or have their work read out.

Commentary

As seen in the lesson last term the class was interested, articulate and willing to contribute to the discussion. This has the makings of an interactive classroom. At all stages the pupils are brought into the learning experience. They share ideas, discuss together, offer alternatives and evaluate each other's work without prejudice. All the pupils in the class were, at some time, either asked or offered to contribute ideas and opinions, although there is still, I think, an over-reliance on about six pupils to move the discussion on. They are very open, and when asked if they liked the exercise were quite happy to say 'No' if that is how they felt. Those few pupils were able to give reasons for not liking it.

The pupils were always given thinking time and there was frequent use of talking partner groups. I still feel that these groups are a bit large (about six each) to ensure all the pupils get a fair opportunity to voice their opinions.

When asked to offer success criteria, these came readily and with confidence, which showed that their opinion was being sought regularly.

Again there was an excellent response at the end of the session.

Suggestions for extending good practice

Your relationship with this group remains strong. I am sure you will miss them next year. I suggest that their receiving schools be made aware of what they can achieve.

The pace of the lesson was good and, although a bit breathless occasionally, time was given for the pupils to think. I would suggest you revisit the talking partner groupings, and either make them smaller (maximum of three), or make them more formal on occasions by introducing a chair, scribe, etc. I think this group would respond well to this.

Extending the use of peer marking would also work with this group. Getting them, in pairs, to check each other's work against the success criteria, and putting two or three positives plus one suggested improvement, would give them a great opportunity for deeper thought and discussion.

An extension activity that could work with this group would be for each of them to write a plan for a narrative, and then swap it with someone else who would be responsible for writing the piece to that plan. The more you can encourage this group to share and engage in discussion the better.

The practice of creating their own success criteria is well developed and should be encouraged in all areas of the curriculum. Their example could be shared with the rest of the school.

Thank you for sharing this stimulating group with me again.

Year 9 History

The lesson was taught by an initial teacher trainee, attended by the class teacher. This summary highlights five of the 'Ten things to be clear about', and rounds off with an evaluation of how well AfL strategies are contributing to successful teaching and development.

Intention

Displayed on the whiteboard and pointed out during the lesson, was the key question: *How did Hitler use his total power?* The instruction for the main task was: *Explain what Hitler did and expand on the aspects identified.*

Interest

As pupils came in, they willingly joined in the discussion of their recent experiment, sharing responses to the fact they'd drawn a swastika / Sanskrit peace symbol in their books. They also remembered items from a recent assembly and previous lessons. All of this, and subsequent behaviour throughout the lesson, indicated a high degree of engagement in the topics.

Success criteria

Remembering, thinking and making connections seemed to be key. Also noting things down and explaining points of detail were prominent, but implicit.

These were not made explicit. No distinction was made between historical processes and content specifics relating to the topic involving Hitler. It was not made clear whether it was more important to remember details involving Hitler, rather than to develop the skills of remembering or explaining. Or were concepts such as 'absolute power' 'dictatorship' etc. most important? There may be multiple objectives, including appreciation of democracy and 'citizenship', alongside historical skills and topic content. How can the objectives usefully be made clear to the pupils, and how can they actively get to grips with them and develop a sense of ownership of them? This is a good question for action research.

Making criteria explicit would enable the pupils to know where the main focus of the learning lay, and enable the teacher to praise those specifics. That would also enable pupils to self assess and peer assess, which they were not asked to do.

Improvement

There was an implication, I felt, that pupils might try to remember details of the Hitler material, but because the criteria were not explicit, the pupils did not seem clear how to improve.

Application

It was made clear by the teacher at the beginning, and in some conversation with individuals and pairs, that awareness of the issues being discussed enables the pupils to appreciate what it means to live in a democracy and not to take its advantages for granted. This point was not returned to formally, but will probably provide a strong reference point as further lessons continue the topic. Again, explicitness would be helpful.

Signs that AfL is working

Pupils:

- happily come into lessons
- are confident, e.g. talking about each other's work
- are happy to accept challenges
- show respect, e.g. when peer assessing
- focus on their targets for future improvement
- take responsibility and take decisions
- take initiative, e.g. about what they've missed when absent
- set themselves high-level targets, e.g. moving from 'describe' to 'explain'
- offer solutions to problems, e.g. say things like *Could I instead . . .?*
- show independence, e.g. say *This is what I've done* rather than *Is this right?;* ask their own questions, not confined by our questions; take the lead, e.g. log on and show their work to one another
- change the ways they approach their work
- don't go in straight lines, but go where their learning takes them
- think more deeply before answering
- go more deeply into ideas more quickly
- are getting better results
- continue and extend their work outside lessons.

Year 10 Science: two lessons

Lesson 1

This was the last in a series of three lessons on rockets and forces for ten Year 10 pupils with moderate and complex learning difficulties and autism.

What hands-on experience, observation, and decision-making did the pupils engage in, particularly relating to success criteria?

- In the previous two lessons, deciding the success criteria for the activity, recorded on A1 flipchart as:
  - *Following instructions: we will have made viable rockets to fire*
  - *Team work: we will still get on with each other*

- *Understanding gravity and forces: being able to tell someone else about forces and rockets*
- *Staying safe: no-one will be hurt.*
- In the previous two lessons, preparing the rockets in groups of two, three and four pupils, to the point of needing to complete the parachute, putting in wadding, fuel and a motor.
- In this lesson, checking the validity of the success criteria for the activity.
- Completing the making of the rockets, involving cooperation, measuring, dexterity, problem-solving in relation to materials ...: e.g. when packing the wadding and folding the parachute ...
- Finding and marking the rocket's centre of gravity.
- Spinning the rocket on a string to gauge balance.
- Checking safety for bystanders: e.g. *Imagine one of these going in your eye.*
- Helping with the camera to film the events: e.g. *It's less blurred, Miss, if you look through the eye-piece.*
- Counting down to launch.
- Sensory appreciation of rocket firing and aftermath: e.g. *It smells like a double cheeseburger.*
- Suggesting reasons for the relative performance of the four rockets: *Tightness of the cone; Use of black tape which burned; Maybe fire went into the motor.*
- Puzzling about causes for what happened, looking closely at debris, checking evidence ...
- Drawing conclusions from the experiment: *We succeeded in all our criteria; Rockets can be dangerous; Don't pack the body too tightly; The nose cone must not be too tight; We can't answer all the questions we ask; Don't place the launch pad near where people are.*

Lesson 2

This was the third in a series of four lessons on time, distance and speed for thirty Year 10 pupils in a mainstream secondary school. The 'Ten things to be clear about' are used as a framework for observing and analysing the lesson.

1 Making clear how we work together

The pupils appreciate your approach. Your manner is calm, purposeful, and completely focused on the job in hand: in this case, learning how to use time-distance graphs to calculate speed. No time was wasted. When they arrived, you focused them on the aims and started straightaway.

You maintain individuals' attention from time to time by a kind of unobtrusive shepherding: you don't interrupt the flow of what you, or they, are saying any more than to say quietly to a pupil, using her/his name, *This way, _____, We're starting now, _____*, i.e. brief, polite, firm prompts, expecting and gaining compliance.

Timings help to keep the pupils on track. In this instance they had no longer than five minutes per task, and you did not speak to them without interaction for longer than a few minutes at a time either.

You praise them by name for specific positive performance: knowing the meaning of a word, being able to explain, asking a constructive question, etc.

You have enabled the class to use a number of cooperative routines. These included in this lesson: pupils who were absent in the last lesson working with pupils who have finished the previous lesson's task, and, later on, peer assessment.

One of the ways you might consider developing your teaching and their learning further would be by identifying the aspects of attitude and interaction that you might like to promote: for example, their asking of questions. If you wanted this to develop, you would give encouragement by feeding back specifically and positively in the way that you did to the boy who asked the short sequence of questions (perhaps prompted by his having been absent from the previous lesson). You can underline this perhaps by saying something like 'That's good: questioning helps us dig deeper and learn. Let's have more of that, please.'

2 Making clear what we know about this

You asked the class to recap what they knew at the beginning of the lesson, as it progressed and at the end. This is a major teaching strategy for you. They were prompted to recall the preceding practical lesson with the trundle wheels out on the field. The focus was on key words and concepts: gradient, and the relationships between distance, time and speed. The pupils made very effective use of the small whiteboards to show their answers to your questions, for example, interpreting graphs displayed on the interactive whiteboard.

Just before the pupils left the laboratory, they were asked three summarizing questions: *How do you calculate time, given distance and speed, for an object in motion? Can you give an example of a unit measuring speed? What does 'gradient' mean?*

3 Making clear what we are trying to achieve

You referred to the displayed aim *How can we calculate the speed of an object from distance/time graphs?* This and the accompanying lessons are designed to enable the pupils to perform well in the higher GCSE paper, and you used past exam questions during the activities. Sub-questions kept up the lesson's focus and momentum.

When I asked eight of the pupils individually 'Why are you learning these things?' they referred to the exam at the end of next year. When I prompted them to think of other reasons, three came up with employment-related notions of Olympic Games time-measuring and car journey times. See section 10 below.

4 Making clear what might be interesting about this

I don't think this issue was brought to the surface. Of course, in a single lesson it is not possible to make everything explicit. The pupils were certainly interested enough to carry out the tasks. But, if their motivation was overwhelmingly extrinsic and related to satisfying examiners in a year's time, you might consider whether their learning could be enriched by addressing the topic's relevance to matters that might engage them intrinsically. Some open questions of this sort might serve the purpose: 'What do you find interesting or useful about graphs? Does the relationship between distance, time and speed play a part in any of your daily activities or interests?' The point would be, not to drift away from your focus, but to enrich the learning through relevance and extension.

5 Making clear how we know how well we're doing

The criteria for success were inherent in the lesson's aims and the sub-questions that punctuated the activities. Discussing exam questions and the number of marks that might be gained also made this clear.

Your peer assessment sheet (see section 8 below) gives exact criteria.

You might like to consider the potential value of enabling the pupils to define criteria for themselves. For example, could you give them some criteria with gaps and challenge them to 'complete the picture' in a kind of cloze exercise? Is it useful to help them to create the criteria for top-class work? Could you analyse a model answer and deduce the markscheme? The key issue is whether such strategies can deepen the pupils' understanding and give them greater autonomy.

6 Making clear how we are going to tackle it

You dealt very efficiently with practical matters of equipment, checking they all had the whiteboards, pens, paper ... You were explicit about the procedure for the lesson: rehearsing one calculation together first, before they did their own, and then peer marking. You modelled the process and drew out the reasoning with questions. The pupils gave the impression of being sure and purposeful about tackling the tasks. No-one appeared to be adrift or not managing.

Over the series of lessons, the pupils will have used a range of study methods: listening to information; watching a video clip on different modes of transport and their velocities; practical measuring; graph drawing and reading; and so on.

Your approach to breaking down tasks into steps and showing them in action seems well honed and gives the pupils confidence. When I asked a couple of pupils about how they like to be taught, they said they preferred you to model how to carry out tasks, rather than have to work things out for themselves.

7 Making clear what we can do when we get stuck or go wrong

One pupil, early on, asked a series of questions and showed he has no qualms about appearing unsure in front of his peers and you. The method you gave them for performing the tasks was so effective that problems didn't seem to arise.

I wonder how you can try to develop the pupils' self-reliance and interdependence. Sometimes pace in lessons militates against encounters with difficulty.

8 Making clear what we have achieved

You told me how pupils have used traffic lighting in the past to signal confidence and satisfaction with their performance. In your experience they are honest and pretty accurate in their self assessments, not least because they probably realize they'd be caught out by you, or by their peers, if they tried to hide a lack of understanding.

You praised them for correct answers throughout, and told them at the end *You have listened well today*.

The peer assessment sheets you prepared will be used next time. These present precise criteria, first, for drawing the graph:

- *A clear and appropriate scale has been used for the x-axis ...*
- *The x-axis has been correctly labelled Time ...*

and so on, yielding a score out of 9; second, for calculating speed from the gradient of the line:

- *The speed of very slow and slow walking has been calculated correctly by calculating the gradient of the line*
- *All working has been shown in full ...*

and so on, yielding a score out of 3. The marker is guided to summarize by listing two ways in which *You meet these exam criteria really well: . . .* and *Next time you need to focus on: . . .*

9 Making clear how we can improve

The pupils will focus on improvements when they complete the peer assessment sheet, which directs them to decide *Two targets I have set myself to improve my score.*

You keep the focus on the extrinsic aspect of gaining marks, rather than on the intrinsic learning in relation to distance-time-speed and graphs. Is there a way of getting the best of both worlds?

10 Making clear how we can use what we learn

You asked the pupils questions about x and y axes on graphs. You also checked their understanding of what dependent and independent variables are. Would it be useful for them to make connections with other areas of the curriculum, for example, in relation to graphs as a means of plotting relationships? Is there a generic skill in the collection, presentation and reading of data that contributes to the scientific process: is that in fact a crucial reason why they are doing this topic? Is that what you want them to learn, as much as the content about the calculation of velocity? I think this is packed into the explicit aim for the lesson. Can your pupils be helped to develop their own sense of that? What grasp do they have, and what grasp do you want them to have, of what they are learning?

You referred to an aspect of real life inasmuch as *Objects don't often move at a constant speed.* This acknowledged that we simplify sometimes when we treat data: an important lesson about science, and truth and knowledge.

You told me afterwards that the class will go on to do some work involving tachographs and police speed cameras, so the pupils will be able to explore applications of the concepts they are studying. I don't know whether they have a sense of the 'big picture' of the four-lesson topic. If they do, it can inform their engagement in each task.

Reflection A7.1

The strengths and weaknesses of such observations are:

. . . .

. . . .

. . . .

We can give our lesson observations more of an AfL focus by:

. . . .

. . . .

. . . .

Appendix 8
Building resilience and autonomy

Portsdown Primary School in Portsmouth has developed the use of attractive colourful posters. These advise pupils what to do when they get stuck or need to check what to do next. Copies can be ordered and purchased through the school office.

I am very grateful to Daphne Wright, AST and Year 1/2 class teacher, for giving time to share this work and help write it up. She led the design of these visual aids to collaborative and independent learning and the development of their use throughout the school. Impressed by their effectiveness, the local authority decided to provide every school across the city with copies of the posters as a way of supporting this approach to AfL.

The posters pose questions to help learners make progress at the beginning of an activity, after they have made a start, and when they think they may have finished. In each classroom there is one A1-sized poster displaying all three sections. Each of the three elements is also shown on A2-sized cards available to learners on their group desks:

Getting started

- *Do I know what we are learning today?*
- *Do I know how I am going to be successful?*
- *Do I know what equipment I need?*
- *Do I know what is expected of me?*

[Think bubbles refer to L.O. and S.C. (learning objectives and success criteria)]

If I am stuck

- *What do I already know? What did we talk about?*
- *Who can I ask for help?*
- *What can I do to help myself?*
- *What am I aiming for?*

[Think bubbles refer to the Working Wall and S.C.]

When I am finished

- *Have I met the success criteria?*
- *Have I assessed my work using the faces?*
- *Have I asked a partner to check/assess my work?*
- *How can I make my work better? What would I do next time?*

The posters and cards display three self assessment faces: puzzled, neutral and happy. These are replicated in the shape of individual lollipops, which learners in the lower ability Year 1 set and in the reception class can hold up to show how well they understand what they are learning. These have been preferred to a traffic-light coding of red, amber and green, avoiding confusion between a green light meaning 'I can ...' and the 'green for growth' highlighter meaning 'think again'. A crinkly-mouthed puzzled expression was chosen, rather than a down-turned mouth, to reinforce the idea that the focus is not on mood or whether learners like their work, but on understanding in relation to the objectives and criteria.

Ofsted inspectors found that learners knew what the posters were for and made good use of them alongside self and peer marking. They swap exercise books and talk to each other about next steps. Talking partners see work through to improvement, which is then reviewed using the tag *I can see you have ...* The inspection report referred to:

> well planned and practical lessons, which match the learning needs of all pupils. The outstanding teaching motivates and enthuses pupils by supporting them in understanding what they need to improve through clear and achievable targets. Effective assessment systems and procedures inform teachers how to challenge pupils' learning and support better progress. For example, work marked with different coloured highlighter pens indicate to pupils where they are being successful and where they need to improve.

These routines have evolved as whole-school policy. In its early stages AfL hinged on WALT and WILF, which gave way to feedback marking, greater independence in pupils' use of criteria, and their focus on *To be successful ...* One of the first things the teachers, assistants, and the pupils themselves learned to do was to use pink highlighters to show where criteria have been met and green highlighters for areas to develop: 'tickled pink' and 'green for growth'. Other features of AfL included 'working walls', which display objectives, criteria, key questions, examples of work and reflections on achievement and learning.

The quality of the outcome depends on the criteria and clear explanations about how to perform tasks. The pupils were originally introduced to this when working on instructional writing in literacy. A task was set: to write how to make a paper plate. The teacher told them she would follow their instructions to the letter, and make the plate that evening at home. At the start of the next lesson the children had to describe the paper plate they thought they would see. Then they were shown the plate their teacher had produced, and had to identify why and where the instructions had been 'good' or 'needed improvement'. They also had to predict how many areas of 'tickled pink' and 'green for growth' the teacher should show. This proved to be a powerful introduction to feedback marking, which is seen as part of personalized learning in the school.

Here are some examples of written feedback in a Year 2 pupil's exercise book, taken from work over several months:

Checking my friend's work

Assessed by: _____ _____

You have met the success criteria by:
- ***putting your address in the right place***

I found *the address is in the top right corner*

- ***signing the letter correctly***

I found *love from* → *that means she knows him well*

- ***using PS in the right place***

I found *she never put any PS, but she did know where to put it*
   → **Did you talk to her about this?** *Yes I did.*

- ***using the right word at the beginning***

I found *she put the right word which is Dear.*

You could improve your letter by:
having neater handwriting so we can all read it.

You could use *some time to practise your handwriting.*
Good advice!

Responding to my teacher's comments

This is what I did well ...

I used the success criteria well and I asked the reader a question and I used excla-mation marks. I used powerful verbs, like contact, beating and grab. I also said how the prince felt.

To improve I need to *ask more questions like → Why did you go? Did I do anything?*

Next time I will *definitely use similes like → My heart is smashed like a glass, and you are as beautiful as a flower.*

Well done. Has this helped you to think about ways to improve your writing?

Yes it has.

Assessing my work

Using the success criteria, find three things that you did well. Remember to show examples from your work.

- *colourful leaflet –*
  I coloured in my pictures
- *good clear layout –*
  I've got questions and headings
- *technical words and phrases –*
  like respect each other.

Find an area you need to improve next time.

Next time I need to write headings myself.

Well done, you have assessed your leaflet well.
Well done, you have tried to use more formal language as you said you would.

The teachers have found it is essential to look out for the improvement point selected by the pupil last time, and to mention how it has been developed in the latest piece of work. Continuity of comment and effort is thought to be essential.

In this school great emphasis is given to:

- revisiting key skills at every opportunity;

- listening to what the pupils say about every aspect of their activities;
- making concrete use of the feedback pupils give.

These teachers believe that, if they don't model the learning and the task, it won't happen. They try to live by the saying 'Be the change you want to see'.

Reflection A8.1

The strengths of such practices are:

. . . .

. . . .

. . . .

I / We can apply some of those ideas by:

. . . .

. . . .

. . . .

Appendix 9
Examples of whole-school development

Infant school

Background

This school joined the Portsmouth Assessment for Learning project in 2003–4. A pair of teachers attended three training days, one per term. They were visited in school on two occasions by a university researcher. One of the teachers reported in 2003:

> *It has helped me focus on what I am supposed to be teaching. The learning outcome is clearer, whereas previously the activity dominated.*

The teachers found the values underlying AfL were well suited to the school's preferred culture:

> *We have always been positive about encountering difficulty – to struggle is good. All of the children are encouraged to have a go and are not criticized for making mistakes.*

The teachers' view of the effect of being on the project was very positive:

> *The quality of questions asked by teachers in lessons has improved. Previously we answered our own questions without realizing it. Now, with the consistent use of wait time, the children answer. . . . The content of lessons is now focused on the learning intention and not the activity. Planning has become more efficient, directed by the learning intention. . . . You can't change what you teach, but, in order to improve standards, you can change how you teach it.*

Before joining the project, the deputy headteacher had been to a Shirley Clarke training event, and followed that up by practising techniques taken from her books. The Assessment Reform Group's rainbow of ten principles of formative assessment had also been used (see the ARG website, www.assessment-reform-group.org). The deputy headteacher and headteacher looked at 'how it would tie in with where we are as a school'. Over the year of the project, consideration was given to whole-school marking policy. The revision made it positive, constructive, and criterion-specific. Staff members discussed and changed their methods: making learning intentions clear for all lessons; making learning intentions the focus of marking; and giving wait-time during questioning.

The deputy headteacher was also able to explore AfL development across the school in one of her national professional qualification for headship (**NPQH**) assignments. The school's commitment to this work was evident in the decision for a second pair of teachers in the fifth year of the project to participate in the action research. The interest and activity are ongoing.

Every half term the Year 1 team looks at the curriculum and asks 'How could it be better?'

> *We set high expectations for children's attainment, rate of progress, relation-ships, and equally for ourselves.*

Groups of pupils are put together, reviewed and changed in order to support, for example, those who are weak in maths or literacy:

> *We do not keep things as they are. If we've identified they are not making progress then we plan accordingly. We do mind-mapping which helps the children to see where to take the next step. We are focused in independent learning and making choices. All of our children have a voice and take ownership of their learning. We want our children to be lifelong learners.*

There is a whole-school system for termly assessments which feed into pupils' individual education plans. Year leaders in particular, but also subject leaders and the senior management team, are responsible for planning responses to whatever emerges. For example, adjustments are made to learning support assistant provision and to targeting by the special educational needs co-ordinator. This might lead to observation of certain children, more in-depth assessments being carried out, looking at able children, seeing whether planning is in place to stretch and challenge certain children or groups. A whole-school database records termly reading, writing and maths teacher assessments and predicted levels on P-scale and/or the national curriculum. Year teams agree the focus for assessments and moderate standards:

> *We challenge one another to say 'I think it is a level n because . . .'.*

The system enables comparisons to be made across classes, challenging everyone to investigate why certain children might be underachieving.

The school's ethos is significant:

In class we look at children on a day-to-day basis. They have a positive attitude and are eager to come to school. They enjoy telling other people about their learning...

There are opportunities for further training and development. Appointments and promotions are made with all of this in mind.

Evaluation

The school's development can be mapped using these three questions, cross-referenced to the 'Ten things to be clear about':

- What are the strategies being used?
- What are the benefits?
- What is the evidence?

At this school these AfL strategies were seen in action during lessons:

- establishing and maintaining an ethos of working together and helping one another, e.g. whereby pupils have roles to perform as a contribution to the smooth running of lessons [1];
- teacher presenting herself as a learner alongside the pupils [1];
- re-visiting and building on existing and recent knowledge, skill and understanding [2];
- clear description and display of learning objectives, referring to them throughout activity, and inviting pupils to do likewise [3];
- explaining the rationale for activities [3];
- openness to unintended outcomes and readiness to modify expectations in the light of what is discovered through activity [7];
- enabling pupils to make choices and take decisions according to interest and preference [4, 6];
- teacher modelling skills and joining in skilled performance [1, 3, 6];
- encouraging pupils to talk about their thinking as a regular way of working [1];
- encouraging pupils to decide things for themselves [1];
- pupils used to a sequence of activities involving them in cycles of practising, showing, reflecting and commenting, discussing and defining possible changes, further practising [1, 5, 6, 9];
- encouraging pupils to check their responses [5, 8, 9];
- guiding and supporting a pupil in difficulty (i.e. not complying), referring to the key criteria and continually leaving him the option to 'come back into the fold' [1, 5, 9];
- space and time to reflect, ponder, wonder [1];

- modelling self assessment and guidance for self improvement [5, 9];
- pupils self assessing [5, 8, 9];
- pupils using highlighters (pink for success) to identify instances of partners' meeting success criteria, when discussing one another's work [5, 8, 9];
- pupils receiving praise from peers in one-to-one partnership [1, 8];
- providing criterion-specific constructive feedback [5, 8, 9];
- giving structured opportunity for group peer assessment [5, 8, 9];
- giving pupils repeated opportunity and guidance to refine and develop what they do [5, 9];
- making a photographic record of performance for later viewing [8].

with **benefits** such as pupils:

- feel secure and generally happy in a cooperative and inclusive environment;
- readily talk about and share their activity and learning;
- 'own' their activity and learning;
- tolerate ambiguity and complexity, avoiding simplistic or rigidly algorithmic approaches to problem-solving and working;
- develop for themselves a sense of how well they are doing;
- have access to models of effective performance as well as instructive guidance;
- build their performance progressively;
- have opportunity to see their activity in a context of healthy living, enjoyment and potential communication;
- have opportunity to learn with and from one another;
- have opportunity to learn kinaesthetically, aesthetically, cognitively and socially;
- have opportunity to develop their own decision- and choice-making.

evidenced by:

- the pupils' polite and friendly behaviour;
- the pupils talking in a focused way about important intellectual, aesthetic and practical elements in what they do;
- the pupils taking responsibility and initiative in deciding how to proceed and what to think;
- the pupils pausing to consider, not rushing to judge or finish;
- the pupils' readiness to show how well they think they are doing in relation to specific criteria;
- pupils' written work;
- photographic records;

- teachers', assistants' and leaders' observations of the pupils;
- visitors' observations and analyses.

Junior school

A junior school's teachers and teaching assistants used the checklist of AfL strategies given in Chapter 1 (and shown as Appendix 1) to review the main features of their assessment for learning. The activity helped share and affirm their regular practice and update policy. Each year team reported to the whole staff, giving cameo illustrations of their practice. These notes highlight aspects which relate to the 'Ten things to be clear about' (see Appendix 2).

Year 3

- ***Self and peer assessment*** *are linked to traffic lights, encouraging the children to assess themselves.*
- ***Modelling*** *is used to show children what they are expected to do and how to achieve it.*
- *If the children are able to* **teach someone else***, it shows they have learned something and understood it: they can transfer the skills.*
- *We give* **think-time***, using* **paired discussion***, before recapping on the last lesson.*

Mixed ability group in ICT: the children were writing about a holiday. One child finished. I showed him how to insert a photo, move and resize it. He then taught another. Then these children **taught others**, *and so on. By the end all the children had been taught this skill.*

In a science lesson the children worked in pairs to **recap**, *then* **presented** *their ideas to the class. They had to group food pictures and packaging in specific categories and* **explain** *their reasoning.*

Top set working on story settings: we read a range of stories with different settings. Pupils then wrote their own. They read each other's work, and asked **'How can we improve** *our writing? How can we make them more interesting?' The focus was on using adjectives to create atmosphere.*

Year 4

- *It's important to talk about* **how we are going to work together***. Children need to be able to work together before they can learn anything. They need to develop the skills to share ideas to help and further their learning. A safe, happy, settled environment has to be the foundation for learning to take place.*
- **Talking partners** *develop the skills of social interaction and listening.*
- *Making* **links with previous work** *reinforces learning, provides assessment, and shows if they are ready to move on.*
- *The way we are clear about* **what we are going to try to achieve** *gives children a voice. Focusing on the learning, key questions, targets and displays gives the children confidence in their work and helps them value it.*
- **Modelling** *helps engage the children, keeping their attention and motivating them. It sets a standard.*
- *Giving* **timings** *helps children* **organize themselves***.*
- *The children know help and support are always there as it's part of the routine. So they* **know what to do when they are stuck or go wrong***.*
- *We help them see* **skills can be used in real-world situations***.*

The top literacy group in literacy had a prompt on the board: writing about the character of an old man. They **worked together** *to share ideas: verbs for how he moved, adjectives to describe how he looked. They pool their ideas.*

Year 5

(Some staff members not present, so reduced presentation).

- *Talking about* **how we can use what we learn** *is key because learning is training for life.*
- *We want our pupils to be independent learners, able to* **think for themselves***, able to make a valuable contribution to our community and country. The children need to know that what they are doing has a* **purpose***.*
- **Groundrules** *are important because the children need to know what is expected.*

Year 6

- *Using* **talking partners** *shows how we value the sharing of knowledge.*

- *Being clear about* **timing** *helps pace and rigour.*
- **Mind-mapping** *reveals 'what I know'. We go back to the mind-map, add what we have learned, and address misconceptions.*
- *Hotseating is a way of giving the pupils* **active roles**.
- *The children can* **model** *for one another how to perform a certain skill.*
- *It is important to* **identify strengths** *because this improves participation.*
- *It is important to* **mark against the objectives**.

In the first lesson on the geography topic of France, we started with 'We are going to be learning about France. **What do you already know** *about France?' We made a thought-shower on the IWB, and used this to decide* **'What would you like to find out?'** *The pupils worked on their own and with partners. They wrote post-its which were put on a map on their desks and then onto the class world map. This informed our planning. At the end of each lesson we ticked off* **what we learned**.

Secondary school

A secondary school AfL working group trialled specific techniques in their own classrooms. They shared outcomes and experiences. They reviewed progress, then planned how to disseminate and promote development across the whole school.

Introducing this way of working in Year 7 across the school

- Meeting for all staff who teach Y7: e.g. as a team, teachers agree:
    - which AfL strategies, e.g. from the list (see Appendix 1), are already in fairly frequent use?
    - why do we want to experiment with AfL strategies? i.e. give ourselves a clear concise statement of purpose and rationale
    - how will we find out what our pupils already know about using AfL?
    - which strategies will some of us introduce that other colleagues are already using? i.e. build on and out from strength
    - which strategies will we introduce that are new to pupils, if any?
    - how will we involve classroom assistants?
    - how will we share experiences and outcomes?
    - how will we collect and share pupils' perceptions of what difference these strategies are making to their learning?

- what changes in pupils' motivation are we looking for, and how will we evaluate?
- what changes in pupils' progress and attainment are we looking for, and how will we monitor that?
- Each department agrees its answers to the above and those are collected across the school by the AfL link teacher.
- Ask Y8 teachers what they want Y7 pupils to have experienced.

Big picture

- Having outlined a new topic/unit/piece of work, discuss why it might be important, e.g. what relevance does it have to the world outside school?
- Make sure part of the learning objective for the next piece of work has a direct relevance to the world outside school.
- Make sure at least one of the success criteria for the next piece of work has a direct relevance to the world outside school.
- Challenge the pupils to see the relevance of a topic/activity/criterion to the world outside school.
- Challenge the pupils to explain what disadvantage they would be at if they hadn't learned that .../if they hadn't learned how to ...
- Make connections between the next piece of work and previous work.
- Give the pupils, or ask them to make, a chart or map showing how different units/topics build to prepare them for qualification/certification.
- From time to time ask pupils why we are doing this.
- Aim to help the pupils move from 'We are doing this because we have to/because you told us to' to giving reasons for activity that refer to their own decisions, their own targets, their own aspirations for life beyond school; collect and share amongst colleague teams such reasons for activity offered by the pupils.
- Tutors/year leaders reinforce pupils' personal rationales for their school/class activities.

Targets for individuals/groups

- Find ways of personalizing pupils' learning objectives and success criteria: e.g.
  - use a section in their exercise books/folders
  - enable the pupils to put the objective in their own terms, e.g. 'I will ...'
  - enable the pupils to clarify how they will know they are successful
  - use talk partners

- have a reasonably short timescale for the reaching of targets
- have a contingency for those pupils who have reached their target and who can now go on to . . ., and for those pupils who need more time and support to reach their target; i.e. develop self help and independent learning routines, as well as targeted support.
- Agree targets with pupils that are focused on processes (decision-making, group work, etc.) as well as content (subject-specific skills, knowledge, understanding).
- In conversation with pupils refer to their targets: e.g. ask them what is going well, how near they are to hitting their target, what support they need to help them hit their target, how they will show they have hit their target, etc.
- Make sure marking gives feedback on progress against targets.
- Make targets a special feature of some, not all, of the work.
- At the beginning of a topic/unit, discuss whether the pupils want a specific personal target in addition to the overall learning objective and success criteria; if so, take time when they have started the first activity to suggest/agree individual or group targets.

Group work, e.g. evaluating each other

- Train the pupils to use specific roles in group work, e.g. chairperson, note-taker, writer, observer, time-keeper, resources officer, lateral thinker, spokesperson, person who checks we're tackling the learning objective, person who checks we're performing according to the success criteria . . .
- Teacher sequences the feedback/display of work by groups, so that the least advanced show first and the most advanced last, i.e. so that the learning builds through the whole-class sharing session.
- Pupils have a few clear success criteria to refer to when commenting on one another's work.
- Pupils have to praise two aspects of others' work in ratio to one comment which suggests how the others' work could have been better.
- Class builds up a chart of how many groups matched the success criteria, so that, by the end of the sharing session, there is a list of the success criteria for the activity with how many groups met each item.
- Class collects comments on what was learned by working in groups and by assessing one another's work: i.e. how does collaboration help our learning, and how can we improve our collaboration?
- Pupils attach post-its to peers' displayed work indicating how the work matches the success criteria for the task.

- Pupils use a markscheme to identify specific successes in one another's work, e.g. using highlighters, ticks, codes (e.g. SC1 = success criterion 1), etc.

No hands up/questions to help thinking

- Teacher tells the class we are going to experiment with different ways of having whole-class discussion; teacher agrees a class statement about discussion work, e.g.
  - what are the advantages of whole-class discussion compared with other ways of working (such as individual silent work . . .)?
  - how specifically does discussion help us to learn?
  - what do we already do well in our whole-class discussion?
  - how could our whole-class discussion be improved to help everyone learn even more?
- Teacher explains s/he will not want hands up to show you are ready to answer or comment, but s/he will ask pupils by name to speak.
- Teacher experiments with naming pupils to speak and with putting consecutive question to a pupil.
- Pupils are encouraged to ask one another questions.
- Teacher asks pupils to pose questions rather than to answer questions, collects questions, and sets groups/pairs to answer them.
- Teacher does not repeat pupils' answers, but builds their ability to listen to one another.
- Encourage pupils to see there are questions which have a pretty definite right/wrong answer, questions to which there are many different valid answers, and questions which we need to explore further because we don't know enough about them yet; e.g. use those different categories of question sometimes to frame future activity.
- Collect what the class knows about a topic (e.g. mind-mapping), and devise together the questions we would like to know the answers to; use those questions to frame activities.
- Use talking partners to prepare thinking about a question before having whole-class discussion.
- Give thinking time on a question, before sharing possible answers as a class.
- Give status to prepared answers by recording them on (white)board/ flipchart; use such answers as basis for further activity.
- Ask pupils to devise, say, three questions to which they think the answer is yes, three questions to which they think the answer is no, three questions to which they think the answer is a statement of fact, and three questions to which they don't have an answer.
- Pupils use individual white marker boards to show answers.

- Pupils show their thinking in front of the class, e.g. using the interactive whiteboard.

Discussing what helps and hinders learning

- Lead session with whole class on what helps and hinders learning: e.g.
  - record statements that have consensus;
  - develop an agreement, e.g. that we will keep the features that are helpful, and do what we can to change the things that don't help;
  - set a timescale for when we will check how we are doing;
  - on that occasion revise the agreement;
  - use the agreement to prompt rewards/credits;
  - use the agreement to provide positive comments on annual reports to parents/IEPs etc.;
  - use the agreement to highlight WHAT WE ARE LEARNING ABOUT LEARNING, in addition to what we are learning about the subject content.
- Make one-to-one dialogue and group feedback reinforce ideas discussed about what helps and hinders learning.
- Use pupils as researchers to observe and discuss what helps and hinders learning.
- Before setting off on an activity, discuss what will help us and what to avoid because it will hinder us; e.g. have those points up on a poster/whiteboard; at the end of the activity check whether we still think the same about what helps and hinders learning, and amend our advice to ourselves.
- Discuss ways of politely encouraging people to do things that help us learn and avoid things that hinder our learning: e.g. draw that up as a groundrules statement.

Theories behind our approaches to developing AfL

- Techniques such as those listed above are designed to enable pupils to:
  - build on what they already know and can do;
  - be clear about what they are trying to achieve through their activity;
  - feel their activity is worthwhile;
  - work constructively with one another;
  - take as much initiative and responsibility in decision-making as possible;
  - use the teacher and classroom assistant as a resource to help them succeed in their activity;
  - see for themselves how successful they have been.

- This is because these features of teaching and learning have been found by researchers to be associated with successful achievement.

Reflection A9.1

The main points of interest there for me/us are:

. . . .

. . . .

. . . .

I/We can apply some of those ideas by:

. . . .

. . . .

. . . .

Bibliography

Arts Council England's *Creative Partnerships*. www.creative-partnerships.com (accessed Nov. 2008).

Assessment Reform Group (1999) *Assessment for Learning: Beyond the Black Box*. Cambridge: University of Cambridge School of Education.

Assessment Reform Group (2002) *Assessment for Learning: 10 Principles*. Available on the ARG website, www.assessment-reform-group.org (accessed Nov. 2008).

Assessment Reform Group (2006) *The Role of Teachers in the Assessment of Learning*. London: Institute of Education, University of London.

Bandura, A. (1997) *Self-Efficacy: The Exercise of Control*. New York: WH Freeman and Co.

Black, P. (2005) Formative assessment: views through different lenses, *The Curriculum Journal*, 16(2): 133–5.

Black, P., Harrison, C., Lee, C., Marshall, B. and Wiliam, D. (2002) *Working inside the Black Box: Assessment for Learning in the Classroom*. London: King's College, University of London.

Black, P., Harrison, C., Lee, C., Marshall, B. and Wiliam, D (2003)*Assessment for Learning: Putting it into Practice*. Buckingham: Open University Press.

Black, P., McCormick, R., James, M. and Pedder, D. (2006) Learning how to learn and assessment for learning: a theoretical enquiry, *Research Papers in Education*, 21(2): 119–32.

Black, P. and Wiliam, D. (1998) Assessment and Classroom Learning, *Assessment In Education*, 5(1): 7–74.

Blanchard, J. (2002) *Teaching and Targets: Self Evaluation and School Improvement*. London: Routledge/Falmer.

Blanchard, J., Collins, F. and Thorp, J. (2004a) *Portsmouth First Class: Assessment for Learning [2]*. Portsmouth: Dame Judith Professional Development Centre.

Blanchard, J., Collins, F. and Thorp, J. (2004b) *Developing Assessment for Learning in Portsmouth City Primary Schools 2003–2004*. Portsmouth: Dame Judith Professional Development Centre.

Blanchard, J., Crossouard, B., Didwell, E. and Thorp, J. (2005) *AfL Progress Report*. Portsmouth: Dame Judith Professional Development Centre.

Blanchard, J. (2006a) *How Can a School's Self Evaluation Form (SEF) Reflect the Effects of the Portsmouth Learning Community (PLC) and the Every Child Matters (ECM) Legislation?* Portsmouth: Dame Judith Professional Development Centre.

Blanchard, J. (2006b) *Progress and Prospects in Assessment for Learning: A*

Contribution to the Evaluation of the Portsmouth Learning Community. Portsmouth: Dame Judith Professional Development Centre.

Booth, T. and Ainscow, M. (2002) *Index for Inclusion: Developing Learning and Participation in Schools*. Bristol: CSIE.

Bruner, J. (1983) *Child's Talk: Learning to Use Language*. New York: Norton.

Carr, M. (2004) *Assessment in Early Childhood Settings: Learning Stories*. London: Paul Chapman.

Clarke, S. (2001) *Unlocking Formative Assessment: Practical Strategies for Enhancing Pupils' Learning in the Primary Classroom*. London: Hodder & Stoughton.

Claxton, G. (2005) *The Wayward Mind: An Intimate History of the Unconscious*. London: Little, Brown.

Csikszentmihalyi, M. (1991) *Flow: the Psychology of Optimal Experience*. New York: Harper Collins.

DCSF (Department for Children, Schools and Families) (2008) *The Assessment for Learning Strategy*. Nottingham: DCSF Publications.

DES (Department of Education and Science and the Welsh Office) (1987) *National Curriculum – Task Group on Assessment and Testing*. London: Kings' College, University of London.

de Shazer, S. (2005) *More than Miracles: The State of the Art of Solution-focused Therapy*. Binghamton, NY: Haworth Press.

DfES (Department for Education and Skills) (2003) *Every Child Matters: Change for Children*. London: DfES.

DfES (Department for Education and Skills) Teaching and Learning in 2020 Review Group (2006) *2020 Vision*. London: DfES.

DfES (Department for Education and Skills) Secondary National Strategy (2007) *Assessment for Learning 8 Schools Project Report*. London: DfES, ref 00067-2007BKT-EN.

Drummond, M.J. (1993) *Assessing Children's Learning*. London: David Fulton.

Dweck, C.S. (2000) *Self-Theories: Their Role in Motivation, Personality, and Development*. Philadelphia: Psychology Press.

Fielding, M. (2004) 'New Wave' student voice and the renewal of civic society. *London Review of Education*, 2: 197–217.

Fielding, M. and Bragg, S. (2003) *Students as Researchers: Making a Difference*. London: Routledge/Falmer.

Fielding, M., Bragg, S., Craig, I., et al. (2005) *Factors Influencing the Transfer of Good Practice*. Nottingham: DfES publications.

Fielding, M., Sebba, J. and Carnie, F. (2008) *Portsmouth Learning Community: Final Report on the Partnership between Portsmouth Local Authority, Portsmouth Schools and the University of Sussex*. Brighton: The University of Sussex, School of Education.

FilmsforLearning: visit www.filmsforlearning.org (accessed Nov. 2008).

Flanagan, C. (2004) *Applying Psychology to Early Child Development*. London: Hodder & Stoughton.

Gilbert, C. (2006) *2020 Vision: Report of the Teaching and Learning in 2020 Review Group*. London: DfES (www.teachernet.gov.uk/publications).

Harris, A. (2002) *School Improvement: What's in it for Schools?* London: Routledge/Falmer.

Johns, M. and Blanchard, J. (2007) *Getting in the Habit: An Action Guide for Teachers*. Portsmouth: Dame Judith Professional Development Centre. (This guide can be accompanied by cards for use in lessons: *Getting good at learning*.)

Keele University, Centre for Successful Schools (1990) *School Surveys*. Staffordshire: Keele University (www.keele.ac.uk/cfss/).

Kelly, A.V. (1992) Concepts of assessment: an overview, in G. Blenkin and A.V. Kelly (eds) *Assessment in Early Childhood Education*. London: Paul Chapman.

MacBeath, J., Demetriou, H., Rudduck, J. and Myers, K. (2003) *Consulting Pupils: A Toolkit for Teachers*. Cambridge: Pearson Publishing.

Marshall, B. and Drummond, M.J. (2006) How teachers engage with Assessment for Learning: lessons from the classroom, *Research Papers in Education*, 21(2): 133–49.

McIntyre, D. (2003) Has classroom teaching served its day?, in M. Nind, J. Rix, K. Sheehy and K. Simmons (eds) *Inclusive Education: Diverse Perspectives*. London: David Fulton.

Mosley, J. (2000) *Quality Circle Time in Action*. Cambridge: LDA.

Polanyi, M. (1962) *Personal Knowledge: Towards a Post Critical Philosophy*. London: Routledge.

Reay, D. and Wiliam, D. (1999) I'll be a nothing: structure, agency and the construction of identity through assessment, *British Educational Research Journal*, 25(3): 343–54.

Royal Society for the Encouragement of the Arts (2002) *Opening Minds: Education for the 21st Century*. RSA (www.thersa.org/newcurriculum).

Sadler, D.R. (1989) Formative assessment and the design of instructional systems, *Instructional Science*, 18: 119–44.

Sadler, D.R. (2002) Learning dispositions: can we really assess them? *Assessment In Education*, 9(1): 45–51.

Sebba, J. and Ainscow, M. (1996) International developments in inclusive schooling: mapping the issues, *Cambridge Journal of Education*, 26(1): 5–18.

Stenhouse, L. (1976) *An Introduction to Curriculum Research and Development*. Basingstoke: Heinemann.

Torrance, H. and Pryor, J. (1998) *Investigating Formative Assessment: Teaching, Learning and Assessment in the Classroom*. Buckingham: Open University Press.

Vygotsky, L.S. (1978) *Mind and Society: The Development of Higher Psychological Processes*. Cambridge, MA: Harvard University Press.

Wiliam, D. (1994) Assessing authentic tasks: alternatives to mark-schemes, *Nordic Studies in Mathematics Education*, 2(1): 48–67.

Winnicott, D.W. (2006) *Playing and Reality*. London: Routledge.

Index